home. Whatever crisis you are going through, this book will help you pick up the broken pieces of your life, put them together, and see who you really are! You are fearfully and wonderfully made in your Creator's image. All the days ordained for you are already written and will be fulfilled. No amount of crisis, rejection, humiliation, or betrayal will change that!"

Florence Nyakundi, founder, Fenny Ministries

"Many of us have had a moment in our lives when we thought, 'I wish I had a therapist to talk to.' *12 Habits for a Sound Mind and Joyful Life* is like an invitation into a safe place with your very own therapist. Through deep and thought-provoking questions and powerful stories from her own life and the lives of those she has cared for in her practice, Diane challenges you to start taking needed risks as you let go of isolation, shame, and negative patterns that have held you back."

Wendy Peter, director, Women on the Frontlines Global

"Broken hearts abound in this day and culture, but so does hope. Hope abounds! That's why we need the healing grace of our Lord Jesus to overwhelm every broken place within us and around us. In her excellent book, licensed Christian therapist Diane Arnold takes us on a journey of understanding what it means to be broken and how we can embrace our brokenness to experience the fullness of God's love. God is inviting you to shed the false identities you have adopted and embrace the truth of who you really are."

Dr. Brian Simmons, Passion & Fire Ministries; ead translator of The Passion Translation®

"When I read a book, I want to know if that person has a heart for people and speaks from experience. I know Diane personally, and I've seen her reach out and touch people's hearts in amazing ways. I love how she drives home profound wisdom with activations and questions after each chapter. I highly recommend you join her in this journey as she helps you to see your heart and identity going from broken to healed."

Ann Tubbs, cofounder, Transformation of the Nations;
president, Hidden Dove Ministries; apostolic leader,
Harvest International Ministries

"In her book, Diane Arnold equips us to challenge the false versions of ourselves. With surprising vulnerability, she discloses how God uses heartbreaking experiences to establish an unshakable identity. The exercises provide practical steps to move from brokenness to wholeness, from despair to joy, and from pain to peace. This book will certainly transform those who have the courage to ask, 'Who am I?'"

Terri F. Burnette, licensed psycho-educational specialist

"All of us have times when we react to the messaging around us instead of living out of a deep sense of personal worth. Filled with real-life examples and supported by extensive research, *12 Habits for a Sound Mind and Joyful Life* is a map and guide to an abundant life. Everyone who incorporates its principles will improve their relationships and their own sense of self-confidence, thereby living a much happier and fuller life. I highly recommend it!"

Stacey Campbell, founder, Shiloh Global

"Keeping up with the pace, pain, and pressure of everyday life has led many of us to this mental health disaster we find ourselves in. In this book, Diane Arnold takes readers by the hand on a hope-soaked journey of self-discovery and shares the freedom God offers and calls each of us to."

Dr. Tim Clinton, president, American Association of Christian Counselors

"*12 Habits for a Sound Mind and Joyful Life* is full of compassion as Diane Arnold journeys with us through the pain of brokenness to discover the keys to healing. Through personal stories, testimonies, scientific research, and the Word of God, Diane offers practical activations that are just that—practical. They encourage us to process our thoughts, emotions, and beliefs, and they help us shift from lies to truth, from being stuck to walking free. Should we make the brave choice to engage, she gives us the tools to help us build a healthy identity. Diane guides us to build joy and remember to be led by God's peace, which will build resiliency that carries us through life's challenges."

Debbie Healy, co–senior leader, Celebration Church OC, San Juan Capistrano, CA

"*12 Habits for a Sound Mind and Joyful Life* is a practical guide to assist readers on the journey to spiritual and emotional health. Diane Arnold is a woman with a strong and vibrant faith that guides every area of her life, and she is also a skilled licensed counselor who understands human nature and the processes that lead to growth and healing. She brings those key areas together as she masterfully provides counseling insights and exercises from a Christian perspective. This book could be the start of your healing journey as you surrender your brokenness to God and allow Him to transform you."

Glenda Hill Nanna, PhD, LPCS, director of graduate counseling programs, Columbia International University

"When Diane placed this book in my hands to read, I was going through a very dark time in my life. I had been betrayed, rejected, and then humiliated. I was in shock and disbelief, brokenhearted and confused. This book gave me tools to refocus my emotions and to learn how to release sadness. It served me as a therapist in the privacy and comfort of my

12 HABITS
FOR A SOUND MIND
AND JOYFUL LIFE

12 HABITS FOR A SOUND MIND AND JOYFUL LIFE

YOUR ROAD MAP
TO OVERCOME
DAILY STRESSES
AND MESSES

DIANE E. ARNOLD

Chosen

a division of Baker Publishing Group
Minneapolis, Minnesota

Published by Chosen Books
Minneapolis, Minnesota
ChosenBooks.com

Chosen Books is a division of
Baker Publishing Group, Grand Rapids, Michigan

Printed in the United States of America

Library of Congress Cataloging-in-Publication Data
Names: Arnold, Diane E., author.
Title: 12 habits for a sound mind and joyful life : your road map to overcome daily stresses and messes / Diane E. Arnold.
Other titles: Twelve habits for a sound mind and joyful life
Description: Minneapolis, Minnesota : Chosen, a division of Baker Publishing Group, [2024] | Includes bibliographical references.
Identifiers: LCCN 2023053926 | ISBN 9780800772819 (paperback) | ISBN 9780800772840 (casebound) | ISBN 9781493447299 (ebook)
Subjects: LCSH: Mental health—Religious aspects—Christianity. | Identity (Psychology)—Religious aspects—Christianity. | Self-confidence—Religious aspects—Christianity. | Christian life.
Classification: LCC BT732.4 .A76 2024 | DDC 261.8/322—dc23/eng/20240328
LC record available at https://lccn.loc.gov/2023053926

24 25 26 27 28 29 30   7 6 5 4 3 2 1

My thanks, appreciation, and acknowledgment to:

My husband, family, and the Family Collective team for all their guidance, love, and assistance with this hope-filled project; Joy Capps, for her work and guidance in polishing and developing this book in its early stages; Brian and Candice Simmons, for understanding and sharing the importance of health and wholeness for the Shulamite bride; all the courageous people who have struggled with appreciating their value and have chosen to walk in restoration and healing.

This material is dedicated to everyone who reads it. My prayer is that it will help you get to the place where you realize you deserve to be loved, known, and understood as a perfect bride.

CONTENTS

INTRODUCTION

When you hear the word *identity*, what comes to mind? Do you think of your career or the name you've made for yourself? Or perhaps identity makes you think about your parental or marital status? Society tells us what our identity should look like and how it should be shaped. But how does that identity relate to us individually? Am I who I think I am, or simply who the world says I am?

12 Steps for a Sound Mind and Joyful Life is designed to guide you in exploring the depths of your true self. Our ability to walk in strong mental health and true joy requires that we first have an understanding of who we really are. This allows us to tackle life rather than look in from the outside.

The wounds we can get in this broken world may weigh heavily on how we see others and ourselves. Through practical exercises and insightful activities, this book will help you pick up the pieces, break through the brokenness, and develop an understanding of who you really are.

I invite you to join me on this journey of truths. Together, we will address ideas like: Where does my identity come from? Why am I truly here? Does my life mean anything in this world? As the chapters unfold, you will see how these questions that we've *all* asked are answered with the one truth that cannot be ignored.

Learn a new script for your life through this journey of inner healing and self-discovery. *12 Steps for a Sound Mind and Joyful Life* will give you the stepping-stones to uncover the answer for who you really are. You are worth that journey. The One who paid the ultimate sacrifice to make you perfect thinks so, too.

We believe in you and want to help you win in this ride called life. So, let's get started so you can start living in continual hope and joy!

PERMISSION AND GRACE
TO TAKE YOUR TIME

Before you get started, please know that working through the various steps found in *12 Habits for a Sound Mind and Joyful Life* is *not a race*.

You have permission to slow down and take your time moving through the material and exercises. In fact, taking your time is going to help you get the most out of it. Each step of this journey has been carefully crafted to help you gain insight into the most important facets of your identity.

With activities that include self-help psychological therapies, journaling, and self-reflection, be especially mindful of what you are learning about yourself, others, and God. Remain open to exploring your strengths, weaknesses, and areas for growth. You may discover parts of yourself that surprise you.

If you are feeling stuck at any point, please be kind to yourself by taking a break and coming back when you feel ready.

Step 1: Restore the Original Me

God has made us what we are, and in our union with Christ Jesus he has created us for a life of good deeds, which he has already prepared for us to do.

Ephesians 2:10 GNT

H ave you ever been in one of those moments where you asked yourself, *Who am I—really?*

One of the stories that best describes this confusing life situation happened to a high school senior named Jill. She was someone I was counseling for what she described as social anxiety.

Jill had a tough time going to class. The other students made her nervous, and she would often end up in a full-blown panic attack just walking the hallways of the school building. She and I spent a lot of time trying to pinpoint what was so hard about going from math to science lab or even to the cafeteria for lunch.

After much exploration, encouragement, and even confrontation with the things that were scaring her, we finally uncovered something interesting. As Jill told it, many of her schoolmates were talking about and exploring actions that frightened her. She found it exciting to listen to their stories of new experiences. It sounded like they were having fun, but it also terrified her.

She would slide into the back of these conversations. After a while, she started thinking, *What would it hurt to try a little ecstasy? It sounds exciting, after all. And what is the big deal about experimenting with my sexuality? They're all doing it.*

At first, Jill needed me just to listen. When she was ready to face some of her worries, we could finally probe more deeply and make some progress. I asked her to describe the panic. We discussed why it felt so scary to try some of these things. As Jill thought more about her fears, her answer surprised both of us. She realized she was disappointed with her friends' behaviors, not her own reactions. She was pretty okay with who she was, and what her classmates were doing felt way outside of her comfort zone.

We spent the next several times together exploring what she wanted to do with her friends, what felt good to her in this season, and what didn't. Jill said she felt at peace when she could make her own choices. After weeks of exploring her thoughts and feelings, she found she could walk the halls of her school without a pit in her stomach and without the fear of being off or of having done something wrong. It didn't happen overnight, and it wasn't all fun and games for Jill as she struggled to understand her true self. However, as she committed to appreciate and work through these healing transformations, she became comfortable in her own skin.

Identity is something we all grapple with at one time or another. It tends to surface the most when we are teens, but it can be an ongoing battle if we let it. It is shaped by a multitude of ideas and factors. Some even navigate between online and offline personas. Our identity comes into question when culture tells us our worth is defined by-

- Popular opinions
- What we look like
- What we wear
- Whom we hang out with
- What we do
- What we accept as truth

During their teen years, kids start asking, "Who am I?" These years are when children learn to explore their independence and, like Jill, grapple with social interactions that significantly influence their lives. I'm pretty sure most of us would say the years from middle school to young adulthood considerably impacted who we are in good, bad, and sometimes ugly ways.

Distinctly Different Characteristics

Most of us are good at labeling ourselves with one or more of the options in that phrase from the 1960s, "The good, the bad, and the ugly."

"Today, I am good because I took in my neighbor's mail." Or, "Today I am bad because I lied to my spouse." Or even, "What I did today was so ugly, it was unforgivable." These labels will often follow us (especially in our minds) as we try to figure out who we are and where we are going in life.

Do you sometimes waver like that between self-inflicted labels of good, bad, and ugly? I know I have. It can touch many aspects of your world when you're unclear about how you think about yourself or something else. Sometimes confusion happens as you reflect on the big picture of life, but more often it rears its head in the little things.

For example, consider weighing two thoughts. *I am unclear about where my kids will get the best education* is very different from, *I am uncertain about who I am or what I was created to do in this life.*

There is a significant increase in fear, anxiety, hopelessness, division, and isolation when anyone uses the wrong benchmark for their identity. When we measure ourselves against unrealistic standards or someone else's achievements, we risk getting to know and understand ourselves as a whole person. The good news is you don't have to navigate this identity journey alone.

I wrote this book to help you uncover answers to questions like: Who am I? What do I want to be in life? What was I destined to do? What is blocking me from knowing and understanding myself? How can I tackle obstacles or dream blockers? I have spent years walking through these hard questions with many people, and I know settling the answers will bring the hope, peace, and joy we are looking for.

While uncovering the answers to these questions may seem like a lot to work through, I want you to remember that discovering your individuality is a journey or process that happens over time. Thankfully, it is not a surprise to God when you get confused. He is ready and waiting to join you in your self-discovery process.

Throughout this book, we will stop and check in with a story that happened thousands of years ago to a young bride-to-be. As we walk with her on this journey, we see her encounter a well-worn struggle of trying to understand her true worth. This young woman was being pursued in marriage by royalty, yet she did not perceive herself as the king saw her—beautiful, whole, healed, and healthy—and this caused their courtship to take many twists and turns. This tale sounds and looks like a Hallmark movie, yet it is a captivating romance found in the book Song of Songs in the Bible. She is referred to in this story as the Shulamite woman.

The Shulamite woman had to walk through a process of transformation and renewal to see herself as the king saw her. It is a picture of Christ calling us, His bride. You and I can walk out the same process and experience the same amazing results.

In the coming pages, the Shulamite woman's break-throughs, along with proven counseling treatment models, will be used to get you to where you can confidently say, "This is who I am, and it makes me happy!" Just like Jill.

Culture Influences You, Me, and Everyone

When it comes to societal impact, age doesn't ultimately matter. We are all affected in one way or another by what others think. In our formative years, culture doesn't seem to have to work as hard to influence our beliefs and feelings about life and the world around us. Take a moment to reach into your memories. Who or what were you listening to when you were growing up? Now search out who and what young people are listening to or watching these days. While authority figures and influences (and accessibility to those influences) may shift over the decades, it is easy to see the pressure in society and how it quietly (and sometimes loudly) continues to shape our lives. For instance, your parents may have turned to their mom, dad, grandparents, and neighbors but now, we have access in seconds to opinions and ideas from every corner of the planet. Some of these may serve us well and help us to grow into the person God created us to be, and others may just confuse us like our friend Jill.

Now, let me be clear: everyone questions their identity at different periods during their life. In fact, stressful times and significant changes will cause you to question many things. Some of those pressures and changes are traumatic, like losing a job, a divorce, personal health issues, or a death in the family. Others are life changers, like the birth of your child, starting a new job, or moving. Since vulnerability makes anyone more sensitive, listening to the right influencer during those critical phases is imperative. (Stick with me, we will work through the best ways to do that in the coming pages and chapters.)

Questioning our identity also occurs when we allow societal influences—such as peers, news reports, social media, cultural values, and accepted norms—to shape us. But seeking value from others is like getting wrapped up in how many "likes" you get on social media. Lots of likes tends to mean you have value, and you are important to the person who read your post or watched your video. Be honest, we have all checked at times to see how many people are following us or have liked our posts. It can be time-consuming and stressful to continue to look for people's feedback. Talk about a never-ending game filled with constant anxiety as you try to please others!

Consider how often your internal worth meter has been thrown off because of something you saw or read. These are the exact moments you need to know deep inside yourself that you are okay and acceptable based on your existing value system. Almost like a car with an original owner's manual, you need to refer back to what you know to be true about yourself.

Whenever life causes you to question who you are, your purpose, or your value, don't ignore it. Whether you are facing a false value system, going through a normal change in life, or walking through a critical stage, there is great meaning in tackling those internal questions head-on. Many of us need help to explore this journey. And that is okay.

It is important to understand that monumental changes, like a pandemic, will make you feel exposed. They are constant reminders of how fragile and interconnected our lives truly are. During those times, some people experience low moods, loss of interest in things, and fatigue. They may also be irritable. If these lingering feelings describe you, reach out to your physician or a mental health professional to talk about ways to work through them.

Research shows that people who are courageous enough to tackle developing their identity live happier and healthier lives.[1] Those who don't address what is happening will likely continue to struggle. The result tends to be more isolation, confusion, or just feeling stuck.

With "you do you" a common catchphrase today, many people are pressured to figure out what that really means for them. We are told that figuring this out is the key to being the "genuine" you. But if you reach for a constantly changing standard or are swayed by the popular opinion of the day, that most likely isn't "you doing you." And you likely won't feel the hope, peace, and joy you are looking for.

These cultural messages remind me of the story of Zacchaeus in Luke 19:1–10. Zacchaeus was short in stature and intensely disliked because of his occupation as a tax collector. One day, Zacchaeus heard Jesus was coming to town, so he ran ahead of the crowd and climbed into a tree to have a better view. When Jesus saw Zacchaeus in the tree, He told him to come down immediately because He was going to his house.

Now, as a tax collector, what do you think Zacchaeus thought of himself? Was he happy with his position in society? Or did he try to hide from the dirty looks and name calling? Like most of us, he probably listened to the words and opinion of others. In fact, it is very possible that Zacchaeus not only believed what people said about him, but he also took it on as his character.

It is easy to see how Zacchaeus probably thought Jesus would not notice or acknowledge him. Even the onlookers were confused when Jesus said, "I'm going to stay at your house today." *Really? Jesus is going to stay with the tax collector? He should be staying with one of the respected Jewish leaders. How could Jesus stay with a person who no one even likes or respects?*

Here's what's extraordinarily cool about Zacchaeus's story. If you look up Zacchaeus's name, it means "pure" or "innocent."[2] As a tax collector, Zacchaeus did not live up to the definition of his name. But Jesus looked past the negative label by calling out his true identity. Jesus recognized who Zacchaeus was and who he was created to be. I believe He is waiting and desiring to help each of us with this same question.

Why a Healthy Sense of Self Is Important

A healthy sense of self is important for all of us. Having identity confusion—believing anything outside of who God says you are—can evoke a roller coaster of emotions. God wants you to understand that you are far more than your Facebook likes. You are more significant than your business titles and worst failures.

In his book, *The Sacred Journey*, Brian Simmons states, "We need to fill our mind with the truth of how God sees us. Others will always judge us by our greatest weakness, but God sees the glory of His Son shining in us. Since His love is an eternal love, it will not end the first time we fail. His love for us endures forever."[3]

Other people's expectations, and your own, can derail you and move you away from who you were created to become. After meeting Jesus, it is certain that Zacchaeus was changed; he lived a very different life. This encounter helped him believe who God said he was and who he was chosen to become.

Questioning your sense of self may be stressful, but it can be a good thing in the long term. It requires courage, vulnerability, and self-reflection to go there. However, facing wounds and twisted messages from your past can bring up pain *and* permanent restoration.

Like the Shulamite woman in the Song of Songs, you may sometimes find this journey difficult or time-consuming. In chapter 1, verse 8, the bridegroom says, "Listen, my radiant one—if you ever lose sight of me, just follow in my footsteps where I lead my lovers. Come with your burdens and cares. Come to the place near the sanctuary of my shepherds." Doesn't this sound peaceful and alluring? It does to me. I can understand why she was drawn to it.

This woman seems to be lost. She needed someone or something to follow that she could trust. Like all of us, she needed to hear an encouraging and comforting message.

Why would the bridegroom tell her to follow in his footsteps? Because during this time, he is asking her to come as she is. Lost and broken from life. She doesn't need to create her own hard path. She can walk in the one already made by the groom. In his footsteps, she will learn to grow and mature into the bride he already sees in her. That is what Christ does for us. He is growing and maturing us to be who He created us to be. In the Song of Songs, the bridegroom tells the Shulamite woman to come with her burdens and cares. He does not tell her to be perfect, to get her act together, and pretend like she is something she's not. He says to come with all her troubles, all her junk, and all her imperfections. Most of all, to come with her questions and concerns.

Just like her, you and I can attempt to understand how drawing close to God will help us understand our true value.

Right now, make up your mind not to let society's standards dictate who you are and what you should like. Instead, take this twelve-habit journey with me today and learn to have confidence and lean into God for wisdom, guidance, and direction.

A better version of yourself is still not God's perfect plan for you! Full restoration means returning to the complete person God created you to be.

Step 1 Exercises: Stop Struggling, Start Restoring

1. In many cultures, it is customary to tell people what you do for a living before you share anything else. Some may even offer what their parents did, where they grew up, or where they currently live. Think about this for a minute: With these statements and explanations, are we genuinely verbalizing the true core of who we are?

   One way to uncover who you are and share it with others is by asking yourself some hard but important questions. Pause for a few minutes and record answers to the following questions:

   - What am I passionate about today?
   - What are my family values that I want to keep in my own life?
   - What is my long-term destiny in life? How about the next five years?
   - What is my current role in society? What do I want it to be?
   - What are my spiritual beliefs? What do I want them to be?
   - What do I want to be known for after I'm gone?

   Keep your responses handy so you can revisit, review, and revise them over time. Don't worry if you do not have the answers to all these questions yet. We will be working on that together.

2. Like Jill earlier in the chapter, exploring and understanding how you actually feel about a situation, person, or comment is key to reconciling your own values or opinions. Consider some of the following messages you may have heard. Write down how they make you feel as you say them out loud. Feel free to add a few messages of your own.

   • You are what you do.
   • You are not lovable unless you have lots of likes.
   • Your success depends on how much money you make.
   • You are not valued if you are not creative in your endeavors.
   • You are different from (or the same as) your family.
   • Acceptance is important.

   After you've written them down, talk with a friend or family member about the good, bad, and ugly influences these messages have on your life as you try to understand who you are.
   If you don't have someone you feel comfortable talking with about these things, let me encourage you to write them down in a journal and talk to God about them. He's right there beside you every step of the way. And, just like Zacchaeus, He wants to spend time with you.

3. Choose one or two positive messages about yourself that you either already know are true, or ones you

want to learn to believe, and write them down. For example:

- I am enough.
- I am a survivor.
- I am fortunate.
- I have realistic expectations of myself.
- God's opinion of me is more important than others' opinions of me.
- I am more than what I accomplish.
- I try to show everyone love, joy, and peace.
- I am a trustworthy friend to others.
- I am beautiful inside and out.

Do any of these messages give you peace? A sense of purpose?

Take some time to be in God's comfort zone today. What do I mean by that? In Song of Songs 1:4, it says, "We will run away together into the king's cloud-filled chamber." This is a place where we can go and feel intimacy and love. I like to see it as a nest of warmth and safety.

To get to this place, spend some time searching for and journaling Bible verses that help you better understand His love for you.

Step 2: Unwrap My Purpose

We have become his poetry, a re-created people that will fulfill the destiny he has given each of us, for we are joined to Jesus, the Anointed One. Even before we were born, God planned in advance our destiny and the good works we would do to fulfill it!

Ephesians 2:10

Has anyone ever told you that you were good at something, but you secretly wondered how they could possibly see you as gifted? You questioned how they couldn't see what you already know—that right in front of them is a person barely making it most days. I have been guilty of exactly those thoughts. Have you?

The truth is that we all have something we are good at doing. For some, these talents come quickly and easily. For others, like me, getting to a place where we feel confident enough to use those skills has taken years.

Early on, my friend Cindy knew she loved working with animals. She considered being a veterinarian but was worried about tackling the required medical training. So, she worked part-time at a nature habitat in the summers. At the same time, she went to school and earned a biology degree. She eventually applied to law schools to become an environmental attorney focused on animal habitat protection. This process took her many years and had several twists and turns. The end result was she found what gave her purpose and joy. She discovered something she was created to do.

Unfortunately, another friend, Shara, had a totally different experience with her love of animals. At one point, she decided she would open a doggie daycare. Shara successfully secured a loan that allowed her to build a beautiful facility. But she soon found out she did not have the skills to care for the animals. Adding to her startup expenses, Shara had to hire groomers, medical help, and boarding assistants. She also quickly realized she needed to advertise. Much to her dismay, Shara soon discovered there were two other boarding facilities within five miles of her new building. The following year the economy became more challenging. She eventually had to close the doors and sell the building. It was a costly lesson for her to discover the need to build a full financial plan, to recognize and gain the right skills for the business, and to see the need for networking and training people she would need to run toward her dream.

A great example of the need for outside preparation and development is also found in the story of Moses. He is considered one of the greatest prophets in Judaism. Most of us would rather not wait until we're eighty, but that was how old Moses was when God called him to do what He created him to do. Moses' journey took him from a baby in a basket, floating in the river, to royalty in a ruling land. From a regular sheepherder to the rescuer of Israel. Moses progressed from someone uncomfortable with public speaking to one of the most powerful people in speech and action in history.

What is really remarkable is that God did not alter Moses' life plan just because Moses could not see it for himself. When Moses had doubts about his ability, God did not tell him, "That's okay; you can stay in the background."

Amazing things happened in Moses' growing and learning journey when he cooperated with the process. The God of the universe gave him step-by-step goals to accomplish, and opportunities to succeed, as he moved into his purpose as the deliverer of God's people.

Feeling Unqualified

If you are like me, there are times when you feel less than qualified or struggle to see life the way others see it. Moses' life story provides us with a good example of walking out our identity or purpose in cooperation with a heavenly Father who loves us greatly and wants us to succeed. Most of us do not comprehend what plans this perfect dad has deposited deep inside us before we were even born.

Psalm 139:13–14 (NIV) tells us

> For you created my inmost being; you knit me together in my mother's womb. I praise you because I am fearfully and wonderfully made; your works are wonderful, I know that full well.

Even when Moses did not see it himself, he was being prepared for the purposes he was designed to accomplish in his life. God desires that we have life goals, be adaptable, and overcome challenges. He wants each of us to fulfill this potential!

A recent research study by George Barna tells us that 75 percent of twenty- to fifty-year-old adults are still searching for their purpose in life.[1] This surprising statistic is one we all need to pay attention to closely. It is extremely hard to know who we are when we do not know our purpose.

Maslow's Hierarchy of Needs is one of the most well-known theories of human development (see image below). Its basic concept is that we all grow through stages in our lives. Maslow observed that humans struggle to move forward to the next level of the hierarchy until the needs of the previous level are met. Ultimately, he believed skipping a level would cause the crisis of being unfulfilled or incomplete. In other

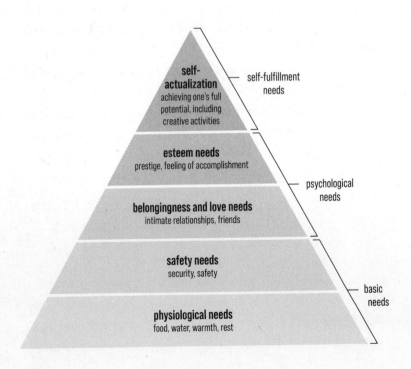

words, missing a step would cause you not to have the skills necessary for your next level of tasks.

For example, according to Maslow's model, people will struggle with understanding the level of community and belonging until they have figured out the level that includes basics of food and shelter.

In Maslow's pyramid, basic life needs are at the bottom of the pyramid, and more high-level dreams and desires are at the top. He proposed that most of our basic life needs are about ourselves, and our higher-level needs involve our relationships and life purpose.

George Barna's research also found that only 33 percent of the twenty- to fifty-year-old age group have found the balance of knowing and enjoying their life purpose.[2] People who are confused about their purpose may struggle with the same problem as Shara from earlier in this chapter. They may have put their higher-level dreams before some of the lower-level basic life needs.

We all enjoy having a place to live, food to eat, and a family and community to help us feel loved and accepted. We need to understand that it is not wrong that each of these needs and levels take time, effort, and energy to develop. When we skip some of these lower-level needs and jump into higher, self-fulfillment needs, we can often find ourselves stressed physically, emotionally, and spiritually.

Struggling with Purpose

According to the Barna study, a large percentage of us are struggling with why we are really here. The majority of us are wondering, *What am I supposed to accomplish or be a part of in this crazy world?* This lack of fulfillment causes feelings of emptiness, disappointment, and frustration.

Maslow's theory tells us that determination and dedication are both necessary for working through all our developmental stages of life. Cindy and Shara are a great example of understanding and committing to the process where your creativity can provide for you, as well as encourage you emotionally and fulfill you spiritually.

Many scholarly definitions tell us our identity involves our beliefs, values, sense of self, the security of our relationships, and understanding of our experiences. It will take commitment and willpower to understand and make sense of these attributes. That is what we are going to do with the habits in this book, so stick with me on the identity journey that leads to a sound mind and joyful life.

Ask yourself, *What am I called to be or do in this world?*

Understanding Your Identity

Let's look at a few recommendations to understand the stages in Maslow's personal development model. As you spend time on these, they will push you toward the end goal of really knowing who and what you were created to become.

1. Know you have access to God's identity promises. Knowing you will never walk this life journey alone can make you feel special, loved, and safe. Maslow tells us that from this position, we can explore and develop through life stages in a healthy way.

Finding and embracing God's promises became my goal when I was healing from a betrayal in my life. In my times of deep struggle and prayer, I felt the Lord show me where to search. He would whisper to me that I was struggling because I was looking for my purpose and identity in all the wrong places. *I felt Him show me that my identity and life purpose resided in my spirit.* This realization sent me on a journey to understand what it meant to have an identity in a place that felt hidden and guarded in my being.

I had to work hard to trust my spirit before leaning into my intellect and emotions. We are often told to follow our gut, but I wasn't sure if that was the same as following the Spirit in me. I learned that I had to spend time with my Creator to understand how and why I was created. The easiest way I knew to do this was to listen to and read what the Spirit said was true in God's Word.

In the second chapter of the Song of Songs, the Shulamite bride begins to see herself in a place of acceptance and love. She starts to understand the importance of the king's opinion. She learns to place this above her more temporal thoughts, emotions, or feelings.

In verse 1, the bride says, "I am truly his rose, the very theme of his song. I'm overshadowed by his love, like a lily growing in the valley!" The Shulamite bride is beginning to see herself as the king sees her, to realize she is the one who brings pleasure to him. That means she is the one who has fully won his heart. She finally understands the level of importance she has with him. She is fully known, entirely accepted, and fully loved.

Since we are all designed to be God's Bride, these thoughts apply to us, too. Knowing how God feels about us becomes very powerful once we learn to accept it. Father God desires this same intimate, identity-revealing relationship with each of us. This is where we begin to understand deep in our spirit that His love continually overshadows us.

When our emotions or thoughts run our lives, we often lack the peace and joy we desire. We can be left wondering how a person can experience this love and acceptance with a holy God. I don't know about you, but I often worried if I was okay with God because I lacked Spirit-level peace. The Spirit needs to take precedence in our lives. When He does, a place deep inside us will be satisfied that will also fulfill some of our basic and psychological needs on Maslow's hierarchy. In this step, spend time asking Him to talk with you about His purposes for your life. Try to rely on your Spirit first.

2. Know you are safe, and you belong.

The need to belong, and the fear of not belonging, are very natural for human beings. In Maslow's hierarchy, the need to feel loved or belong comes right after assuring our safety and security. While most of us want close connections, our insecurities can cause us to resist these relationships. We often feel the contradiction of needing community in a culture that values and celebrates independence.

Are you afraid of exposing parts of your personality that others might not like or might misunderstand? You may be worried about showing weakness or uncovering your true self to people, but did you know that this may prevent you from truly engaging in your relationships? This can include your relationship with God.

A well-known French mathematician from the 1600s, Blaise Pascal, described what many of us struggle with in our lives. He said, "There is a God-shaped vacuum in the heart of every man which cannot be filled by any created thing, but only by God, the creator, made known through Jesus."[3]

It is one thing to be in awe of God, but quite another to be in a relationship and intimate with Him. It is good to know who He is, but even better to feel completely safe, understood, and known in His presence.

In Song of Songs, the Shulamite bride is starting to get a glimpse of who she is called to be. She feels so loved and understood that she starts to think of herself in the same way the king does. She even risks using the same name he does—calling herself *his rose*. She has begun to understand her value is unshakeable to the king. There is nothing that could happen to her or around her that would make her feel unloved. Think of the security in that statement. I am loved and adored—on my good and bad days. No one can take that connection away.

We need to remember that God created us. He knows us inside and out. Since He is omnipotent, there is no greater power in the universe. There is safety and belonging in this statement. God does not make mistakes and is very intentional in the good things He has created in you. In this step, ask Him to feel that safety, security, and value you desire. Get vulnerable in this step.

3. Understand your natural skills and talents.

Each of us has God-given skills and talents. These talents permit us to grow and develop on several different levels of Maslow's pyramid. Our natural skills can provide us with the security of food and shelter. In addition, when done well, they can also allow us feelings of accomplishment.

If you are struggling to understand the talents and skills in your life, a great place to start exploring is by taking a personality test. Three of the most popular personality tests are the DiSC®, Birkman®, and the Myers-Briggs Personality Type Indicator (MBTI®). You can find more information about these and many other options online.

Personality tests identify areas in your life that could be further developed, or strengths that deserve attention. For example, if you were raised in a home that has given great value to higher education, many of your family members may work in the field of education. But if you have always been drawn toward working with your hands, you may feel like you don't measure up to family expectations. Taking one of these tests might help you see that you are better suited to go into carpentry, construction, or engineering rather than become a professor like your mom or dad.

Many people dismiss the importance of looking for life opportunities as they work toward understanding their purposes, callings, and goals. For example, if I were looking to improve my photography skills, it would be valuable for me to look for possibilities to gain experience or understanding by volunteering with a local professional or taking some classes to improve my competence.

It is great to admire talented people, and it is important to set goals that stretch us, but if you don't put forth the effort to make your dreams happen, they won't. Setting measurable goals will help you seek out and prioritize the skills and training necessary. These experiences will, over time, enhance your mastery and knowledge to allow your passions to become a reality.

We each have been given an assignment in this world, and it is one of our highest calls to seek it out, understand it, and work to complete it well. In this step, I would challenge you to commit your mind and heart to pursuing what you were created by God to accomplish.

Step 2 Exercises: Moving Forward with Purpose

1. Answer the following questions about your direction and identity:

   • Is there a level on Maslow's Hierarchy of Needs pyramid where you feel you might be stuck? What would it take to move forward?
   • What are you passionate about in your personal and professional life?
   • Do you feel you have a specific role that you are called to in society? What do you think that consists of today?
   • What do you want to be known for after you have left this world?

2. Spend some time working through the following questions regarding your current relationships and community:

   • Do you feel connected to some of the people close to you?
   • Do you think *they* feel close to you or distant? Why?
   • What are three things you could do to expand your circle or connection with your community?

3. Being proud or inspired by something in your life can benefit your spiritual, emotional, and physical well-being. What areas could you work on in your life to

help you achieve a greater sense of accomplishment? List at least five things that would make you feel successful in some area. Take time to think about or pray through each item you list. Here are some ideas to help you get started:

- Climb a mountain.
- Pay off a big bill.
- Read your Bible from start to finish.
- Work on a skill needed for your dream job.
- Travel to your dream country.
- Volunteer somewhere that inspires you.
- Eat healthy six days in a row, then for a full month.
- Learn how to play chess.
- Try a workout that challenges you.

When I was fifty, I thought I could do high-intensity workouts with some of my twenty-year-old friends. I paid for it with a messed-up knee and shoulder. It wasn't practical for me at that point in my life. While it is admirable to want to stretch yourself, learn from my lesson and make sure each goal is realistic for your season in life.

4. Ask at least one other person to tell you what they see as some of your best attributes and talents. If they are open to it, return the favor by telling them their best qualities.

Step 3: Silence Shame

> They looked to Him and were radiant; their faces will never blush in shame or confusion.
>
> Psalm 34:5 AMP

Most of us, at some point, will experience a traumatic life event. Some of us will go through several. Years ago a crisis in our home rocked my world. Sharing my story has helped me learn a great deal about the real me. It brings cathartic healing every time I talk about this: when shame became a teacher that changed my life forever.

My husband and I had been married for close to twenty-five years. We were building a new house, my husband was getting promoted routinely, and the kids were in a school they loved. I had good friends, a wonderful church, took care of my health, and enjoyed our community. On the outside, things appeared to be going really well.

But inside our home, my husband and I were struggling. It was common for us to avoid talking to each other even when we were in the same room. We argued about the same things over and over. Both of us needed to win so badly that we could not hear the other. Wisdom would have told us to seek help. But out of embarrassment or pride, we decided to ride out the week, the month, the years. And unfortunately, the worst thing that could happen to a marriage did happen.

Neal met someone who spoke positively to him and made him feel desired and important. Their connection turned physical, and he became skilled at hiding it. I didn't find out until he announced one evening that he was moving out and I was not to know the location. In the next few weeks, I discovered that not only was he leaving me for another woman, but he had decided he was in love with her. Needless to say, many things occurred during the next several months. Most importantly, my neat little life came crashing down.

Hiding in Plain Sight

At that moment in my journey, one thing I did not understand was how much I really needed people and support. I needed to trust people to take care of me. Even though I desired that, I never let it show. I was hiding in plain sight. When I was out and about, you would never have known that I was crumbling on the inside.

I remember going into my closet and sitting behind a bunch of clothes. I attempted to breathe, tried to clear my mind, and cried and cried. I didn't realize how symbolic that secret hiding place was for me. I was truly shaken by the loss, and I was worried and afraid. But weirdly, I was also ashamed.

I desperately needed comfort, care, and companionship, but I did not trust I would ever find that in my life. My husband and I had not provided that for each other for years. I began to believe I would have to live without love, care, and empathy. And, with his affair, I began to adopt the idea that maybe I did deserve it. When people internalize shame as I was, the disgrace and humiliation become "who you are." Worse than that, you believe others have the same judgment of you.

Emotions in the Orphan's Heart

Shame is one of the most painful emotions we humans experience. When you feel shame, it is usually some form of self-rejection. Your thoughts are often negative and self-condemning. Sometimes people find their minds go blank, or they feel confused. Other people might experience an upset stomach or nausea.

At its core, shame is the belief that something is intrinsically wrong with us. Shame can make us feel that we are not enough and we don't measure up. And then what happens?

Our hope turns into hopelessness.

Our power becomes powerless.

Our worth becomes worthless.

The bottom suddenly drops out of our security.

When this heightened level of shame is present, we often pull away from others. Even from those who love us most. This experience is called having an orphan spirit, which Jesus described in John 14:9–10. The orphan's heart[1] feels alone, unprotected, and unable to depend on others.

Brené Brown, a well-known author and researcher, has spent most of her life studying the topic of shame. She tells us that if you could put self-disappointment or shame into a petri dish and add to it empathy and unconditional love, shame would not survive.[2] Why? Because these components would disintegrate shame.

So if what Brené Brown discovered is true, here's a tough question: If we all have the unconditional love of Father God, and maybe even empathy of others in our lives, why don't we feel it? Why is the shame still hanging around us? Why do we still struggle to believe that someone even really cares? Why is it so difficult to let others or God into our hearts, emotions, or circle of trust? That struggle with shame was the arrow buried in my heart, and it caused me to hide.

In my personal journey, I learned that many things could keep us from God's unconditional love, care, and the freedom those give us. Our painful circumstances can become hindrances. People can become roadblocks. It can inhibit our personal growth or ability to take new risks. One of the biggest walls when struggling with shame can be our own thoughts and feelings after a shame-inducing incident. It could be we hurt someone with our careless words or actions, got into financial trouble, failed a class or a project at work. People who have been abused often find themselves wrestling with feelings of self-doubt. Most of these experiences stop us from experiencing God's empathy, unconditional love, and freedom.

In my own attempt to stop hiding and overcome what held me hostage in the closet, I followed three specific steps. These included:

- recognizing the symptoms of shame surrounding me.
- learning to be vulnerable again—purposefully.

48

- risking and leaning into healthy love experiences in my life.

Where Shame Started

Before we explore how each step works, let's take a look at where shame started. Genesis 2:9 (NIV) says:

> The LORD God made all kinds of trees grow out of the ground—trees that were pleasing to the eye and good for food. In the middle of the garden were the tree of life and the tree of the knowledge of good and evil.

But there was one rule in the garden: don't eat from the tree of the knowledge of good and evil. Genesis 2:16–17 (NIV) makes that rule clear:

> And the LORD God commanded the man, "You are free to eat from any tree in the garden; but you must not eat from the tree of the knowledge of good and evil, for when you eat from it you will certainly die."

We also see in verse 25 what things were like under that rule: "Adam and his wife were both naked, and they felt no shame" (NIV).

Why did God mention that they felt no shame? I wonder if it was because shame would become one of our culture's biggest problems. I think it is also likely that God wanted us to know that from the very beginning, shame was not part of His normal daily plan for us.

Interestingly, the Hebrew word for shame, *bosh*, is a lot stronger than just being embarrassed. *Bosh* means to be utterly dejected and bound with a sense of sin and guilt.[3] With one simple action—disobeying God and eating from the fruit that was off-limits—both Adam and Eve went from walking in the garden, talking to God, and feeling peace and joy to experiencing utter dejection.

In Genesis 3:9–13 (NIV), the story continues:

> The LORD God called to the man, "Where are you?" He answered, "I heard you in the garden, and I was afraid because I was naked; so I hid." And he said, "Who told you that you were naked? Have you eaten from the tree that I commanded you not to eat from?" The man said, "The woman you put here with me—she gave me some fruit from the tree, and I ate it." Then the LORD God said to the woman, "What is this you have done?" The woman said, "The serpent deceived me, and I ate."

Most people hone in on the finger-pointing in these verses. Few people drill down to the fact that Adam and Eve admit to their fear and hiding, yet they never express guilt for eating the forbidden fruit. They don't admit responsibility for doing what they wanted and not listening to what God said was good for them. They could have spoken the truth at that moment: "We were hiding because You told us not to eat the fruit, and we chose to do it anyway." But rather than confess what they *did* and admit their guilt, they tried to hide *who they were* and continued in shame.

There are times when shame can have a purpose in our lives. It lets us know when something is not right. The shame I am referring to throughout the book isn't short-term and it isn't beneficial. It is a continual reminder of being devalued.

It is what keeps us from right choices and from being who God created us to be.

Healing from Shame

When we try to hide who we are, or our identity, it can be because we are struggling with shame. It is important to start your healing process by recognizing that shame.

My personal journey was long and difficult. It was hard on me as well as our three young boys. My husband moved to an apartment, and we both started the legal process of separation. At times it was gut-wrenching to realize that all our lives were about to change and there was no looking back. If you have ever been through a betrayal, you understand that working through the hurt and humiliation are only a part of the process.

Our first Christmas without Neal was a moment of adjustment for our little family. The boys and I were starting to get used to being without him daily in the home. It was heart-wrenching, but we were making a new and very different life together.

During that same time, the Lord was stirring Neal's heart. He said he sat alone in a church service on Christmas Eve and knew he had made the biggest mistake of his life. He was positive none of his family would want him back in their lives. After the holidays, he asked all of us if he could have another chance. The boys were all-in, and I was willing to try.

Our initial "trying" looked a lot like a blame game. We were convinced if the other person would just get it together, there would be peace and joy going forward. Shame-based people struggle with being vulnerable with their faults. But hiding makes it impossible to be genuine or vulnerable. We try to control our environment to keep others from getting too close to the truth, from encountering the real us.

In Song of Songs 2:9, the Shulamite bride also hides. This verse tells us, "Now he comes closer, even to the places where I hide. He gazes into my soul, peering through the portal as he blossoms within my heart." The bride realizes she has built a wall between herself and her groom. He felt the distance between them. In hiding, she has let her past shame block her intimacy with her lover.

Sadly, she has been shutting herself off from the very thing that could help her heal. But then the groom looks deep into her soul, seeing all of her hidden places, and he doesn't retreat. He gazes into her innermost being, moves toward her, and lets her know she is loved.

The Power of Honesty

After recognizing shame, the next step is learning to be honest about your hurt and pain. Shame's power can create fear and brokenness in your life.

Isaiah 54:4 (NLT) confirms the need for transparency with its hopeful message:

> "Fear not; you will no longer live in shame. Don't be afraid; there is no more disgrace for you. You will no longer remember the shame of your youth."

Mark 5:25–34 tells us of the woman with the issue of blood. She had struggled with bleeding most of her life, and her problem made her an outcast. According to the law, she wasn't even allowed to be in public. When she heard about the miracles Jesus had performed, she made a plan. She snuck out of her house and went to the marketplace to find Jesus. She finally located Him in the middle of a thick crowd. Determined, the woman pushed forward to touch the hem of His garment. Instantly, Jesus felt power leave His body and turned around to ask who had touched Him. Since so many people surrounded Him, the disciples had no idea who it was.

But she knew. Jesus was talking about her.

> Then the woman, knowing what had happened to her, came and fell at his feet and, trembling with fear, told him the whole truth.
>
> Mark 5:33 NIV

This woman took a huge risk. She knew that she would be disgraced and possibly even punished once those in the crowd realized they had been exposed to her uncleanliness. She was living in constant shame. Yet even knowing what would happen to her, she stepped forward and confessed that she was the one who had pushed through to touch Jesus.

Despite the woman's fear, she moved *toward* Jesus rather than away from Him.

That is such an important note, and one I needed to see. It felt safer to keep hiding and controlling who got to hear parts of my narrative. But it is a risk that needs to be faced when dealing with our shame: Are we willing to become vulnerable again with people and perhaps even God? Do we understand that it is a *strength* to push forward even though we risk being hurt—possibly for a second or third time?

Risking Vulnerability

How did Jesus respond to the woman who reached out to touch Him? His first word to her was *Daughter*. He called her His daughter. In Hebrew, the phrase "daughter of God" means "acceptable to God, rejoicing in God's peculiar care and protection."[4] With one word, Jesus said she was loved and worthy.

Did you hear that? Not only was she healed, but she was given her real identity—daughter: accepted one, cared for and protected. With one word, He removed from her any fear or blame for her actions. She was separated from who she believed herself to be.

When we allow ourselves to be known, we are well on the way to experiencing the freedom of a shame-free life. Much like the Shulamite bride, the Lord already sees everything about us and approves. We are acceptable to Him. We are His daughters and His sons. We are cared for, protected, His bride.

When we are ashamed to admit that we need healing or ashamed to admit that we've been damaged, that can cause even more shame. That's precisely what happened in my life. It is no secret that when you're suffering from shame, the last thing you want to do is make yourself vulnerable. In fact, the reason you might be suffering from shame is because you took a risk with someone! So why would you want to open yourself up for more?

Shame doesn't always come with huge hurt or betrayal. It can sneak in through the most innocent and unexpected ways. Sometimes by just being different.

- You may have a different ethnicity than your friends or family.
- You may be shorter or taller, larger or smaller than friends or family.
- You may have been born with great poverty or great wealth.
- You may have been abused by the people who were supposed to love and care for you.
- You may have some characteristics often associated with the opposite sex.
- Your family may just be different, a little odd, or not present in your childhood.

No matter where your shame comes from or what your ultimate goal is, *it will take some risk* to overcome. If you want to experience connection with others or even with God, taking steps to make it happen will require you to take chances and be open to sharing.

We live in a culture where making yourself vulnerable—exposing your fears and uncertainties and taking emotional risks—is considered a form of weakness. Most of us want to run away from these emotions. But when we open the door to genuine connection and healing by exposing ourselves, we have those intimate experiences that bring purpose and meaning to our lives.

Leaning into Love and Acceptance

The third step we need to take to heal our shame is to literally lean into love and acceptance.

Unfortunately, the enemy knows if he can get us to hide ourselves from who God made us to be, we will lose sight of our identity and the love and acceptance we desperately need.

Think about this in conjunction with what we see happening in our culture right now. For instance, the online world often takes the place of us being more physically relational. Frequently our lives are held captive by schedules, phones, and computers. Because of that, we are constantly distracted and don't have time to focus and build genuine rapport with others. Consequently, we are less relational, more isolated, and less likely to experience closeness to others.

We may know these close encounters, or *unconditional love experiences*, are essential to health and healing in our lives. But if we are being realistic, we also understand they involve taking risks and effort on our part. We will talk more about this in the next couple of chapters.

Stop Being Afraid—Start Taking Needed Risks

We run into Mary of Bethany only a few times in the Bible, but we see her at Jesus' feet every time. Her risk and devotion were the ultimate experiences after receiving love and acceptance. She could feel it from Jesus, and she wanted to be close to Him whenever she could.

In our encounter with Mary in Luke 10, the Lord defends her when Martha, her sister, rebukes her for leaving her in the kitchen to do all the work. Martha was frustrated that all the prep work was on her shoulders alone. Have you ever been the one left to take care of the mess while someone else gets to be at the party?

While Martha was complaining, Mary sat with the disciples listening to Jesus teach. She was experiencing a relationship, connection, and love. Scripture tells us that Martha was anxious and concerned about many things. The housework may not have been her only complaint. Yet Jesus' response in Luke 10:42 reveals his approval of Mary: "Mary has discovered the one thing most important by choosing to sit at my feet. She is undistracted, and I won't take this privilege from her."

The "one thing" Mary had chosen was time with God, in His presence. She prioritized an unconditional love experience. She knew she had lived a life of shame and embarrassment. (She is believed to be the "sinful woman" in Luke 7:37–38 who wet Jesus' feet with her tears, wiped them with her hair, and anointed them with costly perfume.) Now, she was a different person in the presence of love and acceptance.

Shame cannot exist in the presence of true love.

Hiding in the closet, I was afraid to let those love experiences in. I remember asking God to show me that He even cared about all I was going through. I asked Him to show that He was protecting me and providing for me. I was hoping that He would do both of those things in a way I thought it should look.

But instead, He answered by filling me with incredible peace; a peace so powerful, it did not even make sense on most days. He showed me He loved me by sending people over to connect with me, bring me meals, and pray for change and healing. And He answered my prayers in another important way.

Both Neal and I were able to push past the anger and mistrust to find common ground. God was working on both of our hearts. I trusted God, and He told me to not rush, but to have patience in this journey. We were blessed with a group of faithful friends that took on the mission to cover us weekly in prayer while we waited. The process was filled with many highs and lows. We both needed considerable patience, perseverance, and unconditional love to overcome the damage we had inflicted to the relationship. But we both chose to trust God in the process, and we are so glad we persevered. God restored our minds and emotions and healed our marriage!

The words you hear when someone speaks, or even when you read a book, are often forgotten. But when Father God speaks His love to you, His truth becomes a part of you in a way you will always remember. If you are feeling the same hurt, I pray you let Him meet you as He did me.

The Shulamite woman heard this same message in Song of Songs 1:16. The more she experienced God, the more glorious He became in her mind and spirit. His love will release that knowledge directly to our hearts. Lies and mistrust told her to stay guarded and to hide from Him. In these interchanges of love, she discovers His tenderness and caring toward her. As she is washed by this love, her response is simple. She speaks the words, "You are pleasing beyond words."

In *The Sacred Journey*, we are told that Jesus is willing to leap over mountains of fear and walls of insecurity until He has captured our hearts.[5] (How incredible is that?) What do you think would happen to you if you truly understood how loved you are by the God of the universe, how special you are to Him?

Step 3 Exercises: Evaluate Your Shame

1. Think of a time when it might be helpful to listen to shame. Write out what that felt like as you walked through the experience.

2. Reflect on a time when listening to or getting caught up in shame actually got in the way of doing life. For example, shame could have kept you isolated from others. Write out what happened.

3. What do you notice about your thoughts when you are feeling shame? Do your thoughts race, or does your mind go blank? Journal what happens to you. Are you aware of what you are telling yourself during these times? What would unconditional love tell you?

4. How do you think you physically appear when you are feeling ashamed? If someone were to see you, how would they describe you? For example, are your eyes downcast? Are your shoulders slumped? Write out what happens, so you can increase your awareness of how you carry yourself during shaming episodes.

5. We have talked about how shame makes us want to withdraw and hide. Think of a relationship in which your reactions to shame may be interfering with developing a deeper interaction with someone you care about. Describe what has been happening. What do you need to change in order to make this relationship healthier and more fun for both of you?

Step 4: Let in Love and Acceptance

Instead of your shame you will receive a double portion, and instead of disgrace you will rejoice in your inheritance. And so you will inherit a double portion in your land, and everlasting joy will be yours.

Isaiah 61:7 NIV

Several years ago, I counseled an amazing woman who taught me some important lessons about the value of love and acceptance when dealing with shame.

Sarah was what I would consider a live wire. She had long ago given up her opportunity to celebrate who she really was and what she was destined to complete here on earth. She spent a lot of time projecting who she wanted to be. She was clearly disturbed and agitated when we first met in my office. She had obviously spent most of her life looking for a fight. I felt like she used our initial conversations to try to unsettle me with stories of her past behaviors.

As I pondered her statements over the following weeks, I realized she wanted to get the rejection over with and out of the way. She was convinced that I would not like her if I knew all of her bad and ugly history. I found out later she expected me, along with others in her life, to be so disappointed in her that we would all abandon her.

One day she walked into my office, laid her head on the back of the chair, and blurted out, "I have something else to tell you that you can't fix. I had an abortion when I was in college." I just listened as she continued, "I knew my boyfriend and I were too young to get married. I knew it went against what I thought about life. But the baby wasn't convenient, and we didn't know what else to do."

Then she started sobbing. "I came in today to have you help me get rid of the shame. I have kept this secret for a long time. The regret and pain of this decision have been my constant companions for over twenty-eight years."

As she took a breath, I reached over and touched her knee and prompted her to continue by saying, "How about we spend some time talking about it now?"

My heart broke for Sarah because she, like many of us, had heard a popular message from culture: "My body—my decision." The problem with that worldview was that it had caused her constant pain. Now she mainly had contempt for herself and many of her decisions. I have met many Sarahs who wished they would have known what it was like on the other side of their choices.

Sarah stated she was not sure she would have changed her abortion choice. But she would have liked someone to help her think through the possibilities so she could have had insight into the future repercussions. Fear and shame had driven her to isolate herself and walk out the consequences alone. And she had kept everything bottled up inside for close to three decades.

Sarah, like me, needed to understand and feel relief, grace, and love in her life. By accepting ourselves for who we really are, mistakes included, we can move past the feelings of regret and self-doubt. Without grace, shame can consume us.

Everyone Has Secrets

In 2019, a research study found that emotional and physical problems are compounded when people keep their shame a secret.[1] In fact, secretive people in general are more depressed, shame-prone, anxious, and sensitive to the judgment of others. They may resort to lies to avoid situations that might expose them.

Secrets often reflect our false beliefs about ourselves. This type of secret shame is unhealthy and an attack on our whole identity. Everyone has hidden something at some point in their lives. But secrets that create shame are the ones that scream "I am bad" rather than "I did something bad."

It is important for us to feel whole and secure. Why? Because we fulfill the call on our lives only out of a place of intimacy and safety. We need to feel the freedom to take a risk. And we need to lean in close to people and even God as our safety-security net in situations when we make a mistake. In short, it is in those *unconditional love experiences* that we start to become who we were created to be.

Unfortunately, secrets reinforce the idea that you must go through life's struggles alone. When you are ready to risk vulnerability, find people who are willing and able to support you patiently without judgment or criticism, who will help you reach places deep inside. They will comfort you as you realize that God not only loves you, He likes you—imperfections and all.

Pruning and Refining Leads to New Growth

If we are going to really understand and experience love in our lives, we need to get to a place where we are ready for pruning and refining. While I was sitting in my closet, God was talking with me about my life choices; at the same time, He was addressing issues with my husband. A season of getting rid of the dead things in our lives, like our guilt, rejection, and hurt, is necessary for the new growth of a sound mind and joy.

It is important to know that feeling sorry for the messes we've made in our lives is key to our pruning and healing. A true turning from our past mistakes may be hard and even painful, but it will help us grow and change. What kind of change? The change that brings healing and acceptance of unconditional love experiences.

The Shulamite woman feels this in Song of Songs 2:16, where she says, "I know my lover is mine and I have everything in you, for we delight ourselves in each other." She has (finally) been won over with acceptance and unconditional love. Her groom saw her in her hiding, and she has now reached back out to him.

The Song of Songs reminds us that we never cease to be loved by God in our struggles. He does not forget about us. He always loves us. First John 4:18 (NIV) reminds us of this with "There is no fear in love," and that perfect love, which is what God has for us, drives away fear. Romans 8:1 also tells us He takes away all condemnation, through Jesus. Those who know the love of God have nothing to fear.

Humiliation Is Baggage That Grows in Secret

Guilt, shame, and humiliation over past events and choices are some of the baggage that we carry into our lives and our relationships. It can result in behaviors such as perfectionism, control, isolation, and even hardened hearts.

For those who are married, it can hinder healthy communication with your spouse. For those who are single, it can incumber our capacity to allow people to get close to us. For those of us who have children, it can impact our parenting. And, for those who struggle in friendships, it affects our ability to accept others as they are.

Guilt, shame, and humiliation can affect your capacity to be vulnerable and to believe you are truly loved. These deadly demons evoke an array of painful, discouraging, and untrue emotions. They can make you feel like no one can be trusted—including yourself. I have discovered by some of my own messes that when you have trouble trusting yourself, it is a sure sign that you are struggling with your identity.

Discover Deep, Abiding Love and Healing

Guilt, shame, and humiliation will result in negative self-talk, which in turn can produce a lack of trust and a need for hyper control (in an attempt to keep from being hurt again). In my case, I was determined to be self-sufficient and self-protective. I became an overachiever to keep myself from being vulnerable to the pain of humiliation again. I was stuck in a vicious cycle. I did not have confidence in myself or others to care for me, or to have my back.

Therapists often mention the right and left sides of the brain when talking to people about trust. The different sides of the brain have distinct circuits that become predominant early in life and process information in very different ways. Both are needed to combat negative experiences with trust and regret.

The left side of your brain houses systematic and logical thought. It is more adept at verbal tasks involving analytical thinking, numbers, and reasoning. People who trust only when it makes sense are typically left-brain thinkers. This side of the brain responds well to the truth of the written word to help remind you what your spirit already knows.

The right side of the brain is best at expressive and creative tasks. Right-brained people are often described as being more emotional, intuitive, and creative. They can be classified as freethinkers. This part of our brain helps us to change our perspectives when we are stuck. Right-brain thinkers usually feel trust only when they believe someone is really on their side.

Consider these left-brain reinforcement truths from God's Word, along with a few quotes:

You Have a Destiny.

"'For I know the plans I have for you,' declares the LORD, 'plans to prosper you and not to harm you, plans to give you hope and a future'" (Jeremiah 29:11 NIV).

"The only person you are destined to become is the person you decide to be" (attributed to Ralph Waldo Emerson).

You Have a Purpose.

"Your eyes saw my unformed body; all the days ordained for me were written in your book before one of them came to be" (Psalm 139:16 NIV).

"No one can make you feel inferior without your consent" (attributed to Eleanor Roosevelt).

You Can Make a Difference in the World.

"Being confident of this, that he who began a good work in you will carry it on to completion until the day of Christ Jesus" (Philippians 1:6 NIV).

"You can't go back and change the beginning, but you can change the ending" (author unknown).

Now, contemplate the strength of the right side of our brains. Allow yourself to experience the emotions as you read the statements below.

- *I am destined to live like this—to—I am determined to no longer sit at the gate of humiliation.*
- *I can never trust people in my life—to—I can risk opening up again.*
- *I can never change—to—I won't accept the way I am as my lot in life. I will step up and make alterations where I need them.*

Overcoming Past Pains

As infants and children, we learn and experience through our five senses, which is a right-brained activity. But by the time we leave high school, we are considered primarily left-brained processors. Both sides of our brains use healthy experiences to combat past negative, hurtful experiences.

To combat the mistrust in my own life, I needed to learn to battle the lies, understand my over-triggered emotions, and lean on the unconditional love of God. When armed with these skills, I was able to contend with the fear, doubt, insecurities, deception of the world, and my own mind.

Sarah wrestled with letting herself off the hook for her mistakes. She struggled with trusting that others could forgive her for taking matters into her own hands. Unfortunately, she was also stuck believing she could never forgive herself.

Forgiveness is important. Research in the past couple of decades has shown that forgiveness can lead to improved self-esteem, greater productivity, reduced anxiety, and lessened depression.[2] And those are just the emotional properties. Forgiveness can also have positive physical health benefits. *Strong's Concordance* shows forgiveness is mentioned in 102 verses in the Bible. That is a lot. Clearly, God wants to send us a message.

Like Sarah, forgiving ourselves can be challenging. But if we don't forgive ourselves, it is likely that we have not truly believed God can forgive us, as well.

Did you catch that? Let me say it again. If we don't forgive ourselves, we will likely not truly believe God has forgiven us.

You may have failed many times in your life, but *you* are not a failure. And you cannot do anything on your own to remedy your shame and guilt.

Step 4 Exercises: Your Love Plan

Take a moment to work through the following exercises. Write out your responses somewhere so that you can review them later.

1. Write down the names of a couple people you are ready to talk to about your shame story. Determine how much are you ready to share. Do you want them just to listen and be supportive? Or do you want them to give you their opinion about what you share? Before you start, let them know what you're looking for.

2. Next, take time to consider some lies you are believing about yourself that block you from feeling loved. Write down a few of them.

3. Now that you have explored the lies, spend some time looking for the truth. Work on putting down the opposite or contradiction of the lie. Even if you can't believe it right now, look for alternatives to your initial reaction. For example, I may believe the lie right now that I can't be accepted by anyone or I'm not lovable. The truth is there is nothing we can do to stop the love of God in our lives. So I write down the truth that He completely loves me, and He is perfect love.

   It might be helpful to look in Scripture and see what God says about you. If you do not have a physical Bible, you can find a couple of good ones online that will allow you to look up verses by keyword (e.g., God's love plan, etc.). YouVersion is one example of a free Bible app.

Here are a few verses to get you started: 2 Timothy 1:7; Ephesians 1:4; 2 Corinthians 5:17; 1 Thessalonians 1:4; Ephesians 2:10; John 3:16; 1 Peter 2:9; Psalm 146:5; 1 Peter 2:24.

If you find yourself believing a lie, remember to exchange it for a new truth, like the ones uncovered in these Scriptures. This exercise will start to change the way your brain processes information.

4. As a counselor, I know that allowing yourself to experience painful feelings is integral to the healing process. But know this: In our place of despair and sadness, our heavenly Father is sad right along with us. The safety you experience with Father God opens the door to a whole new way of living. You will find you are no longer held captive by your past but instead courageously stepping into God's plan for your life. You will be known for your joy and peace, and you will reproduce His healing touch in the lives of those around you. This is called the "beauty for ashes" exchange, found in Isaiah 61:3. God works on our behalf. Nothing is wasted in our experiences—all things are redeemed and turned into victory. These are His promises to us.

If you are ready to live in this freedom, take time to pray through the following prayer:

Father God, please show me if I am holding anything against myself or others today. Show me if there are any lies I've believed about myself that I need to release to You.

Father God, I ask You to forgive me and release me from self-condemnation. I ask You to completely cleanse and cover these actions and beliefs with Your blood and Your love. I thank You for Your unconditional acceptance and invite You to be with me in my heart and spirit today.

Step 5: Confront Rejection

Hasn't he promised you, "I will never leave you, never! And I will not loosen my grip on your life!"

Hebrews 13:5

Junior high school can be an awkward time for most people. A lot is happening in young lives at this point. Hormones are raging, bodies are changing, and belief systems are setting. Some kids start to look like young adults while others still look like children. Boys and girls begin to notice each other as more than just someone to tag during recess.

Unfortunately for me, it was a time when I was taller than most of the other kids in my class. At age thirteen, my body development wasn't keeping up with my height. I felt very different than my classmates and extremely awkward. There were times when I was subjected to name-calling. You may have suffered the same. For me, it became my daily goal to try to stay unnoticed.

No matter what this time may have looked like for you, we all have many emotions tied to our memories of those growing years. Our brain works to store them—both good and bad. I often felt like no one even cared. What's worse than those feelings of loneliness and rejection was the fact that I didn't bother to tell anyone about them.

During the adolescent years, our close attachments can start moving from family members to friends. Finding safe people in either of these groups can become a big struggle, especially if you have been left out or excluded. That was my experience.

I can remember a particular Christmas when my family went to Florida to visit my grandmother. With the temperature around forty-five degrees at the beach, it wasn't one of Florida's warmest. But we were from "almost Canada," so anything was better than the weather at home. This forty-degree upswing in temperature found my family wearing our bathing suits and huddling in towels for an hour to say we made it to the beach.

That experience was funny and sad. But what stuck in my memory most was what happened when I returned to school. I was away a couple of extra days to go on this trip, and I guess I expected to be greeted by friends or teachers who were excited to see me. But no one seemed to even notice that I was gone. I slipped into my class, sat at my desk, and not one person turned around or moved in their chair. I can bring up that scene in my memory to this day. I know many amazing people struggle with similar wounds that evoke feelings and emotions of "What is the point?" or "Why am I even here?" If you have ever experienced these mindsets, you are not alone!

A long time later, I processed what was happening to me and my emotions during that part of my life. As with most middle schoolers, my attachments were moving to a different influence group, my peers. Most of the time, however, I did not feel connected with them. In fact, I felt rejected by them, and because of that, I hid from these same classmates for close to a year. My actions left a massive gap in my life that I tried to fill with unhealthy connections in the future.

Wrestling with Rejection

Many people wrestle with these same impressions in their lives. Their great desire is to be known and loved, yet their world seems empty of close friends and relationships. If this is you, I hear you! Because our nervous systems are wired to need others, rejection really stings. Research confirms that sensitivity to emotional pain resides in the same area of your brain that experiences physical pain.[1] Think about this for a moment. Feeling rejected and not loved can hurt like a punch in the gut.

It is essential to understand the ramifications of rejection, isolation, and loneliness and what it does to your psyche. In short, these negative feelings put your brain into self-preservation mode.

From brain-imaging studies, we know the visual cortex (the region of the brain that processes visual information) becomes more active during times of solitude or hiding. Think of sitting in a dark cave. You would be watching for anything that moved, right? At this point, the brain is looking for danger.

While this is happening, the area in the brain responsible for compassion and human responsiveness becomes less active. Why? Because we are in survival mode and focused on our own needs. In survival mode, we have little time for the problems of others.

Why do our brains have this reaction? Simply put, humans were not designed to be solitary creatures. We were created to survive in community. The need to interact is deeply ingrained in our genetic code.

The absence of long-term social connection causes the same early alarm bells as hunger, thirst, and physical pain in our bodies. When we talk about connection, we mean spending time with friends or family. Time on your phone or computer allows you to interact with others, but it doesn't count as authentic community for your brain. The goal is to spend time together face-to-face.

When you are alone, your awareness of your surroundings increases as you subconsciously look for trouble. At the same time, your responsiveness and need for relationship go down. Both of these things will keep you from wanting to reach out and connect to others.

So sitting alone in that cave, your brain has started to go into isolation mode. If someone would try to join you in your cave, your reasoning would tell you that it is better not to make friends because it might get in the way of your need to survive—it might turn out that those friends are actually enemies. This is true whether you are in a familiar setting or not.

Bottom line, if isolation is playing out in your life, you might believe that you could get hurt by forming relationships with people. This rejection-isolation cycle can create chronic loneliness in a person if left unnoticed. If loneliness becomes long-standing, depression may occur. When you are depressed, it further reduces your desire to try to reach for community. It becomes a vicious cycle.

Courage to Move Forward

There are times when we feel far from God and others. It seems as if they are hiding from us even when we are reaching out and praying for support. This can leave us feeling exposed, forgotten, and rejected. The Shulamite woman surely experienced this in Song of Songs 3:1, where she tells us, "Night after night I'm tossing and turning on my bed of travail. Why did I let him go from me? How my heart now aches for him, but he is nowhere to be found!"

What can we do in times like this? The Shulamite bride is an example of courage in moving out of that place of isolation. In verse 2, she tells us how she handles it:

So I must rise in search of him, looking throughout the city, seeking until I find him. Even if I have to roam through every street, nothing will keep me from my search. Where is he—my soul's true love? He is nowhere to be found.

Rejection will find us asking, "Why have you abandoned me? Why don't you love me? Where are you? Why can't I feel connected to you?" And, like her, we must be willing to search and sacrifice for the place where we feel love and adoration.

Connecting with Others and Feeling Whole Again

Many of us grapple with the natural desire to be associated with others. This struggle happens more often if we have previously known love and experienced the joy it brings emotionally, spiritually, and physically. We understand what we are missing, and we want it back!

One result from the pain of feeling left out can be self-pity. In this place, we feel our only option is to lick our wounds. But the pain of feeling left behind or alone can also positively motivate us to figure out what we need to change or heal. Like the Shulamite bride, we need to search for that secure and loving connection.

So, how do we get to a place where we feel whole in our lives again? Let's unpack how to get there together. When feeling left out and isolated, here are a few things you can do to help lessen the pain:

- Watch for signs of seclusion and avoidance
- Reframe your narrative
- When appropriate, work on forgiveness

1. Watch for Signs of Seclusion and Avoidance

Rejection, conditional love, and unreliable or unhealthy attachments are instigators of loneliness and more rejection. I believe that they are some of the greatest hindrances to a sound mind and joyful life, that can reach back many generations in some families.

Social scientists tell us that feelings of rejection, isolation, and alienation are at all-time highs. In fact, they have reached epidemic proportions.

- 46 percent of Americans report feeling alone or left out.[2]
- Only 27 percent feel they belong to a group of friends.[3]
- Only about half, 53 percent, report having meaningful in-person interactions daily.[4]

So, with all the problems in our culture today, why is this such a big deal? Medical science has discovered that these feelings—left untreated—are both emotionally and physically painful. They can create serious medical and long-term relationship consequences.[5]

When rejection results in seclusion, it increases our odds of early death by 26 percent.[6] A 2018 survey by Cigna revealed that "Loneliness has the same impact on mortality as smoking 15 cigarettes a day, making it even more dangerous than obesity."[7]

Rejection that leads to loneliness increases our blood pressure and cortisol levels, which is a powerful stress hormone in our bodies. And then we can have a sleep problem, as well. Studies have shown that loneliness is correlated with sleep disturbance.[8] In other words, poor REM sleep. Studies have also linked isolation and loneliness to problems such as heart disease, cancer, depression, diabetes, and suicide.[9]

Young people who experience loneliness at college are more likely to drop out, which can lead to poorer economic outcomes. Feeling disconnected and unsupported in a job can lead to low job satisfaction.

Loneliness and isolation due to rejection can also bring about episodes of anxiety and bouts of anger. These are frightening consequences of rejection that can lead to broad social alienation. Rejection or social exclusion can also translate into vicious cycles of animosity. We have certainly seen a rise in hate crimes in our culture today. It is important to understand this connection in order to identify strategies to strengthen our local and worldwide communities.

2. Reframe Your Narrative

The next aspect of rejection we need to consider is how we look at the problem. In the counseling arena, there is a therapy model called Cognitive Behavioral Theory. This theory suggests that most of us have automatic thoughts which create our own impressions about what is happening with people or circumstances. I struggled with negative automatic thoughts in my own healing.

An automatic thought, by definition, is the thought that instantly arises in our minds when we are triggered. Often we are completely unaware we even have these ideas. When these automatic thoughts are irrational or negative, they can be harmful to our emotional well-being.

For example, what jumps into your mind when you have a hard interaction with your spouse, friend, or parent? Is it one of these?

- *I'm no good.*
- *Why can't I ever succeed?*
- *No one understands me.*

- *I always let people down.*
- *I am so weak.*
- *I am so disappointed in myself.*

When we feel left out or abandoned by others, our automatic thoughts can try to explain the pain away. We can rationalize situations with thoughts like

- *Hey, they clearly do not understand how much they have wronged me.*
- *There is something seriously wrong with that person.*
- *Someday, I will have the opportunity to get even with the hurt they caused me.*
- *Why does this always happen to me?*

A few months ago, I was on the phone with my friend Temar as she talked a little about her life and some areas of doubt and fear she had recently overcome. One of the things she said was that she was very thankful for the "gift of rejection" in her life. Of course, that caused me to stop. What did that even mean? Why did she see rejection as a gift?

What she shared was amazingly profound. Temar said when she felt rejected or isolated by people, it gave her the opportunity to ask herself

- *What am I believing about this situation that may or may not be true?*
- *What do I think are the intentions of that person?*

- *What are some alternatives to those automatic negative narratives?*
- *Have I included the other person's perspective in my narrative?*
- *What would my heavenly Father want me to know about the situation?*

Here is an example she gave. She had organized a coaching group to meet at a building in her city. A significant amount of planning goes with those types of meetings. Several people had signed up and paid in advance. Two weeks before the event, the building owners canceled her space.

To make matters worse, she discovered nothing was wrong with the space. In fact, another event was going to use this area at the very same time. If you are like me, you probably would have cried foul. My mind defaulted to all the legal questions, how the owner was not allowed to prefer one group over another.

But what Temar did was very different. She asked herself what was true about the situation. She questioned her automatic thoughts. *What if the space had made an error in giving me the reservations in the first place? What if this event space planner was not rude but embarrassed by their mistake? What if this space would not have been able to accommodate all my needs?* And ultimately, *How does my heavenly Father want me to respond?*

In the journey toward resolving the situation, she sat down with the hotel representative and discovered serious problems were going on behind the scenes. Due to sound and equipment needs, this space would have been a problem for her group. Fortunately, because she responded the way she did, they were willing to help her financially with new arrangements for a different local space.

Had Temar followed the automatic thought, that they were out to harm her business, it may have caused her to lose the perfect solution. The opportunity to acknowledge her feelings of rejection and intentionally redirect her thoughts and actions allowed her to see rejection as a gift.

3. When Appropriate, Work on Forgiveness

In the past decade, researchers have become increasingly interested in forgiveness and its potential for improving personal well-being. Lack of forgiveness often leads to anger and bitterness and can eventually leak into other parts of your life. Unforgiveness can also cause the same problems with our health as rejection. And, as with most mental health–related issues, it also carries the added bonus of a tendency to put on weight when you are feeling hurt and discouraged.

Holding on to bitterness also has psychological consequences. It can prevent you from moving past trauma and lead to an increased risk of anxiety and depression. Conversely, strong research demonstrates that engaging in forgiveness reduces cortisol levels, lowers blood pressure, reduces cholesterol levels and heart attack risks, and improves sleep.[10] People who work on forgiveness become more optimistic and compassionate. There's also evidence showing that forgiveness increases happiness in your other relationships.[11]

If you are like me, you can often expect people to come and apologize for what they have done wrong. For some type of light bulb to go off in their head to reveal that they've hurt you. We can tend to withhold our forgiveness until that perfect moment. However, forgiveness isn't contingent on another person's actions or words. It's really up to us.

Our minds and bodies are not built to carry the burden of unforgiveness. At the core, forgiveness is the act of releasing a debt. Choosing not to harbor the hurt and anger any longer.

Forgiveness isn't easy, but it's often very healing. And it only takes one person. James 2:13 (NIV) confirms this by telling us, "Mercy triumphs over judgment."

What Forgiveness Is Not and What It Is

Here is what forgiveness is not:

- Forgiving is not condoning or diminishing what the person did.
- Forgiving is not removing the consequences of someone's actions.
- Forgiveness is not necessarily forgetting. Sometimes we should forget, and sometimes we should remember. Remembering helps us to create boundaries that keep us safe in the future.
- Forgiveness is not necessarily reconciling and restoring the relationship. Sometimes things can't go back to how they were. It's great when they can, but it's not always possible.

Here is what forgiveness is:

- Forgiveness is a process to set yourself free from the prison of resentment and bitterness.
- Forgiveness is letting go of our right for revenge.
- Forgiveness is opening ourselves up to receive God's love and to extend that love to another person who has hurt us.

It is essential to understand that this process may take an hour or it may take years. But freedom comes when we decide to walk in forgiveness and love rather than in bitterness and hostility.

Feeling left out and lonely is a negative experience that also may take years to overcome. Unfortunately, it is a normal part of living on this earth with other broken humans. Wherever we deal with other people, we risk being rejected to some degree. In the past, I avoided potential rejection to the point where I missed opportunities to enjoy the people in my life. Please don't isolate and make the same mistakes I made. Dealing with these feelings in a way that allows us to heal our inner selves is a huge step toward establishing a sound mind and a joyful life.

When More Is Needed

In seasons of darkness, isolation, or rejection, we are often forced to see our weaknesses and live by faith. Sometimes during those darkest times, we may need more than the support of others.

I once worked with a man who showed up to his wedding day with great expectation and excitement. However, his bride-to-be had decided to reunite with her previous fiancé. It was a destination wedding, and a horrible mess for him. At first, he was hurt and angry. But as the months passed and we processed the pain together, we became aware of a couple things that were important to his healing.

First, although he wanted to blame everything on his ex-fiancée, he realized that he was part of the problem. He understood that he had contributed to the difficulty of their communication and interaction. He realized the importance of humbly searching yourself when you are feeling left out and lonely, which he felt even during their relationship.

Second, he realized that he needed more than what people could offer him during this time. He needed peace of mind. Have you ever felt that way? No one you talk to, or text with, is able to help you with what you are feeling? In this moment, my client turned to God for comfort.

One of his favorite promises was Romans 8:31–33:

> If God has determined to stand with us, tell me, who then could ever stand against us? For God has proved his love by giving us his greatest treasure, the gift of his Son. And since God freely offered him up as the sacrifice for us all, he certainly won't withhold from us anything else he has to give.
>
> Who then would dare to accuse those whom God has chosen in love to be his?

He said he would repeat over and over to himself that the God of the universe loved him and would not withhold good things from him—ever. If you are feeling rejection, remember these lessons and promises as you work toward your freedom from hurt.

Step 5 Exercises: Leave the Past in the Past

1. Take some time to think back to a situation where you dealt with rejection. Be sure to write out your memories and experiences in response to each question below. (This exercise will work better if the incident isn't too recent, so your thoughts aren't completely clouded by overwhelming pain.)

   • What emotions did you feel as you thought about what happened?

   • Was there something about the experience that made you feel unsafe?

   • What is the narrative you told yourself about the situation?

   • What will it take to move forward to begin trusting again?

   • What is the story you want to tell yourself about this event? How do you want to remember the people and details?

2. Consider closing your eyes and asking Father God to show you who you may need to forgive in this season in your life. This could be something you feel you have already taken care of. Listen for anything that may be brought to your memory.

   If one or more people pop into your mind and you're not sure why, ask yourself: *Is there anything I need to forgive these people for and release today?*

These may be things that have been done or said to or about you. But they could also be beliefs you've had, like

- *I need to forgive them for treating me like they never wanted me.*
- *I need to forgive them for not valuing me.*
- *I release them from never really keeping me safe.*

If you are ready to release an offense in your life, or if you recognize the need to forgive but are having a hard time, consider saying this prayer:

Father, today I want to forgive _____ for _____. I decide to release them from harming me in every way. I choose to bless their lives. Father God, I ask You to free me from the weight of bitterness and offense. I thank You for Your unconditional acceptance and invite You to be with me now in my heart and spirit.

Step 6: Dig New Ditches and Write a Better Story

The LORD your God is with you, the Mighty Warrior who saves. He will take great delight in you; in his love he will no longer rebuke you, but will rejoice over you with singing.

Zephaniah 3:17 NIV

When I was in my thirties, my husband and I lived in a very active neighborhood. There was always a buzz of kids, dogs, and adults moving in and out of each others' houses. One of the neighbors I became very close to had five children, which made having a relationship easy— she always had a child close in age to one of mine, ready to play. What fascinated me most about her was the interactions she had with her six sisters. I only have a younger brother, so it was a very different dynamic for me. I was overwhelmed with a sense of love and community when I watched them together. They had such mutual respect and admiration for each other, no matter what was happening. I was invited to birthdays, noisy holidays, you name it, so I had a front-row seat to see them upset and sometimes very annoyed. But I never saw disconnection or separation.

They knew that they didn't have to be perfect or get along all the time to be safe for each other. At any moment, someone could reach out, and they knew that there would be instant companionship and support. I was aware that this family dynamic was unique, but I didn't understand why at the time. Although not perfect, this family was very secure in their attachment styles (keep reading, I will explain what these are). These healthy connections caused a wholesome dynamic. If one of the sisters felt left out, another one made time to get together for coffee or a walk with her.

I remember my friend saying they rarely let a week go by without one (or all) of them touching base with one another. Watching it was beautiful and made me want to spend more time with her and her family. As I processed their love for each other, I was determined later in life to understand what made them work so well together.

As we move forward toward freedom from rejection, shame, and fear, how do we *stay* in freedom? How do we develop secure, close relationships, like my neighbor had with her family? There are a couple of things I have discovered that have helped me in this area on my journey to wholeness. It starts with what happens in our minds. I want to share them with you here.

How to Create New and Healthier Thoughts

There is a saying in the neuroscience field that goes, "Neurons that fire together, wire together." In other words, the more you run a neural circuit in your brain, the deeper the connection becomes ingrained. Every thought, emotion, and body sensation we have will trigger thousands of neurons and then form a neural network.

I have been told to think of it like a ditch where water flows. As the water keeps taking the same route, the ditch gets deeper and deeper as the soil is eroded. This is similar to how the Grand Canyon formed. With repetition, the connection between a trigger (for example, if a friend didn't return your calls) and a response (worry or anger about the friendship) gets stronger. These neurons, from trigger to response, are wiring together and forming a neural connection that becomes more and more profound.

The quicker I realize that my reaction to the unreturned phone calls is not healthy, the faster I can start working on developing a new pattern. To change this neural network, we have to dig a new ditch: we need to create a new and healthier neural network.

Research tells us we have between twelve thousand to sixty thousand thoughts a day.[1] Research also suggests that approximately 80 percent of these thoughts are negative responses to a situation. And of those, 95 percent are staying in the same ditch or pathway—they are the exact same (healthy or unhealthy) thoughts.[2] These statistics tell us we are facing some very entrenched behavior. But if you find your thoughts on the negative or unhelpful side, it's not hopeless.

There are several things that we can do to make a change in our neural connections.

1. The first thing we can do is work on our health. You often hear about eating better, sleeping better, and exercising.

These are a big part of helping these neurons fire more productively. Better sleep patterns are actually creating space for new neural connections.

2. The second thing we can do is *actively* guard our thought lives. If I keep telling myself my friend is not calling because she doesn't like me or I did something to upset her, it deepens that ditch. The rehearsal makes it stronger. The good news is every time we sleep, our brains have a chance to renew these pathways. Repetition of any thought pattern will cause our brains to assume the ditches are essential and they will be kept. We have to do the work of purposefully changing our thoughts in order to create new pathways.

The Bible tells us to protect our thoughts and emotions: "Guard your heart above all else, for it determines the course of your life" (Proverbs 4:23 NLT). This verse explains why it is important to be careful what we think—there is a lot at stake!

It is critical to know that what we repeatedly focus on will become our "go-to" every time. The Bible tells us in Philippians 4:8 to think on good and healthy things. This instruction is pretty amazing when you realize that through those good thoughts, new super highways of good and healthy thoughts are being built.

> Keep your thoughts continually fixed on all that is authentic and real, honorable and admirable, beautiful and respectful, pure and holy, merciful and kind. And fasten your thoughts on every glorious work of God, praising him always.
>
> Philippians 4:8

We can be purposeful in thinking of all the times when we have felt loved, accepted, and connected, rather than the opposite. Remember what this is doing to the neurons in your brain—not to mention to your emotions and your spirit.

3. After being aware of the importance of guarding our thought lives, the third thing we need to practice is being purposeful about our narratives. What is a narrative? A narrative is a story or an account of events, often told from a specific point of view. Making a new narrative is simply changing how we talk to ourselves. It is how we put new healthy beliefs or reflections into practice, how we build new and stronger pathways.

When my friend doesn't text me back, my new reasoning could be: She is busy but will get to it when she has time. We are good friends; if she doesn't call, I will try her later. Maybe I need to tell her it is important for her to get back to me; phones are not her thing.

To build healthy thought patterns, we need to challenge ourselves to think about something else when triggers arise. Be prepared. Have your new thought narrative ready beforehand. What are some other stories that you can tell yourself?

- *I can accept others for who they are.*
- *My mistakes are not the end; they are the beginning.*
- *I choose to live in joy and live life to the fullest.*
- *I am always good in God's mind.* (See Psalm 139:13–18.)
- *I endeavor to be the best that I can be in all circumstances.*

- *I am a good friend, and people enjoy spending time with me.*
- *God is not punishing me; He is fighting for me.* (See Deuteronomy 20:4.)

Take time to form new narratives and speak these and other life-giving words over yourself and your circumstances. The Bible tells us to do just this in Proverbs 18:21 (NIV), "The tongue has the power of life and death, and those who love it will eat its fruit." We can encourage and affirm ourselves and our circumstances when we have been rejected. And we can do it in our own words.

A 2021 study showed that positive communications may affect all living things. For the study, plants were placed into two groups. One group was talked to daily with positive affirmations: "You are a strong flower. You are going to grow to be healthy and be the envy of other flowers. You will live and not die."

The other group of plants got a tongue-lashing daily: "You are stupid and not loved. You embarrass me with how small you are. Maybe you aren't going to make it as a plant." That even feels ugly to type.

The results showed that the environment steeped in positivity had a significant effect on plant growth. Plants under the influence of constructive words had a higher germination rate, and grew taller, larger, and healthier than those in the negative environment.[3]

In Song of Songs 4:6, the Shulamite bride is speaking life into her circumstances. She has agreed to go to the groom no matter what happens:

I've made up my mind. Until the darkness disappears and the dawn has fully come, in spite of shadows and fears, I will go to the mountaintop with you—the mountain of suffering love and the hill of burning incense. Yes, I will be your bride.

She has finally connected fully with the groom. She heard word after word of affirmation spoken over her (in the previous verses). She feels loved and appreciated by another person. Her trust overcomes her fear. The bride is a picture of the ultimate complete union that can happen as we place our confidence in the King of kings.

The bride is learning not only her identity but her value as a bride. She was created to walk in relationship with someone who is safe and has great things in store for her.

The groom in this story is a picture of Christ, and we are the bride. We are created to walk hand-in-hand with Him. Christ has great things in store for us. He is the Creator of the universe. He will pick us up and dust us off when we fall. He is our safe person. He will never be too busy or have a bad day and not want to be in relationship with us. He enjoys our company, and desires us to enjoy His. Our God will give us wisdom to make good decisions in our lives. He will always be there when we call on Him.

How to Create New and Healthier Relationships

We can fill our lives with people and things that never truly make us whole. Or we can learn to give and receive love in healthy ways, and in so doing, walk toward wholeness and security.

As we've seen, your personal identity—or how you see yourself—is often shaped by your early experiences or attachments in life. If these relationships caused wounds, the emotional damage can sometimes cause you to not understand how to give or even receive love.

Matthew 22:39 tells us to love our neighbor as ourselves. But this commandment can be very limiting if you do not really like yourself. If you do not believe you are lovable, you may find it difficult to receive God's gift of unmerited love and favor. And this will also make it difficult to enjoy healthy relationships with others.

Attachment Theory helps us understand how we connect to people. It tells us the bonding we each experience in the early years of our lives helps determine how we will interact with relationships throughout the majority of our existence. By the time we are twelve months old, we have an established framework in our brain that helps us judge if people are safe and trustworthy. This is put in place through our earliest childhood experiences.

Individuals who experience confusing, frightening, or broken emotional communications during their early childhood can grow into adults who have difficulty understanding their own emotions as well as the feelings of others. Without the strength of positive attachment figures in their lives, these experiences frequently limit their ability to build, maintain, or attach to others in successful, safe, and healthy relationships.

People with secure attachments can be described as *anchored*. They have a favorable view of themselves and others. Their associations tend to be honest, open, and equal. They are comfortable with intimacy. Anchored people are at peace when alone and are not as afraid of relationship rejection. They don't demand allegiance, and they learn to respect the boundaries and choices of others. In relationships, they report greater satisfaction *and* greater vulnerability. They are comfortable with the idea that they need support from others and that people will sometimes require their assistance.

It makes sense that a secure style of relating usually results from a history of warm and responsive interactions from infancy to adulthood. These people believe their partners will provide reassurance and support, so they are comfortable seeking them out in times of need.

If you didn't grow up with healthy attachment models, there is hope! When we are receiving secure interaction and speaking life over ourselves or our relationships, we are building the acceptance and attachment we need as humans. Seeking out healthy people and building those relationships is a powerful means toward healthy change in your attachment style. My neighbor's family permanently changed how I saw healthy relationships. I witnessed how they worked to build each other up with words and actions but were also truthful with their thoughts and emotions.

Jesus is the exact representation of someone with a secure relating style. He was not afraid to make the hard calls in His relationships, even when it meant the ruling social group wouldn't accept him. He didn't seek the approval of man. But He also never tried to control people, even those He was close to. That is still true of His relationship with us now: He allows us to make our own choices and walk of our own free will.

Jesus never doubted who He was or what He was created to do. Doesn't that sound peaceful and refreshing? This description is the identity that God has planned for each one of us. (We will explore this further in coming chapters.)

We need to remember that the pain of rejection is in the past. We can view it as an opportunity to adjust our mindsets about ourselves, to challenge our narratives by digging new ditches. It is important to have compassion for ourselves and bring life to ourselves and the people around us with our thoughts, words, and actions.

Step 6 Exercises: Digging New Ditches

1. Like the story of my neighborhood friend, think of someone who seems comfortable in their own skin. Someone who seems to believe the best about themselves and others. Their healthy characteristics might include attributes like

   - They regulate their own emotions.
   - They have trusting, long-term relationships.
   - They establish effective communication skills.
   - They share their feelings in a healthy way with other people.
   - They don't mind being alone, but they also enjoy social support.
   - They self-reflect about their interactions in partnerships.
   - Their opinions aren't so rigid or weak that they can't be adjusted.

   Which of the above statements do you believe describes yourself? If you can see areas where you would like improvement, which statements would you like to include as attachment goals?

2. Let's figure out some of your negative relationship triggers. Here are examples of things that could be triggers in your day.

- Someone asking lots of questions
- People displaying a lot of affection in public
- People enjoying a lot of time together, or time alone
- Someone with a strong set of values and beliefs
- Crazy or distracted drivers

Think of a couple of your own that send you in a negative spiral. Write them down, including your normal responses to them. Next, decide what your new narrative or healthy response will be in the future and write that down, as well.

When we are speaking life over ourselves or our relationships, we are helping to build the acceptance and attachment we need as humans. Refer back to the secure identity attributes list in number one above. Check the responses you would like to have when negative triggers happen. Don't worry if you slip up. Remind yourself what you want to happen next time, and try again!

Step 7: Navigate Your Loss

My heaviness and tears are more than I can bear. I have spent myself
for you throughout the dark night.

Song of Songs 5:2

Have you ever found yourself completely devastated by sadness and wondering, *What just happened?* Most of us have experienced this kind of curveball. A lot of times, life just does. not. make. sense.

One particular character in the Bible found himself in this boat when he lost his home, family, health, and possessions after a quick series of tragic events. During his season of grief, he actually sat on a pile of ash. The worst part of this story is that he had done nothing wrong to bring on such devastation. It is easy to ask why and think that a tragedy or mess is not justified when you're in the middle of it.

This Bible character, Job, was sitting on the ash pile when a group of friends came to comfort him by being present. They were conducting something called *sitting shiva*, a Jewish custom where for seven days, family members and friends gather in the home of someone who has experienced a loss to lament and grieve with them.

This ancient practice emphasizes the importance of processing loss. At the end of these seven days, the grieving families start returning to their normal schedule, but continue to mourn for several more months.

How Sitting Shiva Helps You Heal

I find it interesting that while a family is sitting shiva, the mirrors in their homes are covered to inspire self-reflection. This part of the custom indicates that it is healthy to go inside yourself and uncover the hurt from your loss.

Friends and extended family are encouraged and expected to honor the pain someone is going through during this time. They come and just sit quietly with the family. In fact, they are told not to speak until the person experiencing the loss interacts with them first.

As a counselor, I know it is hard to find the right words to say to someone when they are grieving. We often hear some of the following unhelpful comments:

- "You got this."
- "God will never give you more than you can handle."
- "Be thankful for the things that are going well."
- "Remember, you are a survivor."
- "There are people who have it a lot worse than you."

Many well-meaning people have added to other people's pain by offering some of these condolences. The sitting shiva tradition is a perfect solution to allow someone to feel the comfort offered, on their own terms. In fact, friends do not speak of the loss unless they bless the memory of the person who passed. This resolves the problem of knowing what to say to a hurting person. I know I have struggled with the right words in this situation. Doesn't it seem simpler to give your friend a hug and tell them you were blessed to know the person they lost? I'm guessing the person experiencing grieving would love to hear the kind words.

We could all learn something from the self-reflection part of this custom. It is a normal impulse to want to avoid or hide from life's hurts and losses. I have heard people who are grieving over experiences with their marriages or family say, "It would be simpler and less painful to just start again." The only problem is that we take all those difficulties, hurts, and traumas with us to the next place or person.

The only real way to heal is to do what the Jewish people do with shiva. To sit, uncover, and experience the hurt and wounds of the loss. Before you run from the pain of the next big life problem, remember healing takes place when you take time to turn and face the hurt. Purposely walking this hard road gives us the strength to climb slowly to a place of healing.

Go Below the Surface

Grief is a normal and natural response to loss. Our body tells us that things have changed. We expect to grieve the death of a family member or friend, but many other significant wounds can also trigger a grief response, such as

- The end of a relationship
- The termination of a job or position
- A move to a new community
- A natural disaster
- A life goal that is suddenly closed to us
- The death of a pet
- When someone we care about gets hurt or sick

Working on your grief is a real opportunity for you to be vulnerable, honest, and proactive in your healing. When you are intentional about understanding and experiencing pain, you can operate from a place of emotional authenticity.

When you encounter your next wound, make a point to be honest with yourself and possibly also with a couple of good friends. Work hard to avoid trying to make logical sense of all that has happened because the grieving process is largely an emotional journey. The road to recovery is often a slow process, so have patience with yourself during your journey.

I tell my clients to release a little bit of sadness at a time. It is like letting air out of a balloon. We can do it slowly or pop it with something sharp. Both ways will eventually release all the air. However, one of those options is gentler on our emotional system and healthier in the long run. To truly heal from a loss, it is essential to take our time and deliberately get to the bottom of what we are experiencing.

An easy way to look at this is to compare it to clearing out water reeds from a lake. Have you ever seen those tall, skinny reeds often near the shoreline? When we were younger, our parents would have us pull them out when they were blocking the dock. We would try to cheat by breaking them off, so you couldn't see them at the top of the water. But eventually they would come back. If we wanted to get rid of them long term, we had to go below the surface and pull them out from the roots.

In our grieving, we can't just deal with what we see. We need to go below the surface and work to mourn what has hurt us. (Yes, it is *work* and sometimes painful to mourn a loss.) Who really wants to run toward that goal when they already feel the shock of the experience?

Loss binds us together as human beings. Grief is a part of life. When you have experienced suffering, it is natural to sense a wide range of emotions. The effects of grief can include feelings of numbness and emptiness. Some may feel angry and annoyed by their pain. In this case, your temper may come out against others for not understanding, or even yourself for not getting over it fast enough. Often, we worry that the grieving process will never end.

Here are a few other things you might be experiencing after a loss in your life:

- Lack of energy
- Headaches
- Times of tearfulness
- Excessive activity
- Sleeping too little or too much
- Eating too little or too much
- Distractibility
- Strengthening of faith or questioning of faith

Processing Your Loss

Grieving, or mourning a loss, is essential because it allows us to release a tiny part of the emotion connected to the lost person, object, or experience. In fact, without the steps involved in the grieving process, a part of us remains tied to the past. This action is not forgetting. Nor is it being consumed by our sorrow. It is a healthy mourning that results in us being able to make sense of our hurt to the best of our ability.

When my husband was only thirty-eight years old, he was diagnosed with stage four cancer. We had three young kids, and his sickness quickly became very real. One of the enormous truths I confronted was, *Will I be raising our boys alone?* This situation caused me to walk through the reality of "for better or worse" early in our marriage. It was an awful and grueling couple of years. It was terrible for Neal to be that sick, but it was also heart-wrenching for me to sit on the outside of that season with him and be unable to physically help. Of course I prayed and sometimes even hollered at God. Even in the yelling, I grieved. At that time, I didn't even comprehend the importance of this step.

Ultimately, I could do nothing but walk with him through the sorrow, and trust God for the outcome. It became a comfort to know I was not alone. As I've watched many of our friends lose this same battle, I am very thankful that Neal was restored. Sometimes our efforts are spent sitting with those grieving, and sometimes we walk through it ourselves. Either way, the grief has to be experienced and processed.

Be Kind to Yourself

There is no right way to mourn and, unfortunately, no quick fix to dealing with and understanding our losses. Although there are no shortcuts, there are pitfalls we can be aware of to lessen the stress and discomfort. Start by learning to be patient and eliminate any self-judgment.

I cannot overstate the importance of being sincere about the feelings you have over the sorrow in your life. In the following chapters, I will share with you a time when I handled this well and another when I handled it very poorly. I was furious at God and yelled about how unfairly I felt I was treated. In reality, I wasn't angry with God, but I was honestly upset that things were not turning out as I had planned. And I was very fearful about the next chapters of my life.

When life doesn't go according to our perfect plan, our necessity to grieve is frequently overshadowed by other feelings that can make it difficult to realize our need to give a little space to healthy sorrow. If you struggle opening this emotional door or the process seems too scary right now, please consider reaching out to a local counselor to help.

I often ask people to begin the process of journeying through a loss by spending time naming the emotions they are experiencing. This activity can be easy or difficult, depending on your emotional vocabulary. Many of us work hard trying to numb or suppress our emotions. A list of feelings might help you to identify yours. You can find a list online by Googling phrases like "feelings list" or "feelings names."

Sometimes it may seem too difficult or scary to address the depth of your loss, but don't skip this crucial step. Taking the time to understand and describe your feelings is the first phase in moving through your experience toward healing.

Next, spend some time thinking about these questions:

- Who or what are you emotional about right now—the situation you find yourself in or an actual person?
- If you are you upset with yourself or someone else, can you name what you feel?
- If you feel numb, where in your body are you experiencing grief? Maybe it's in your head, your chest, or your stomach? Try to get quiet and understand if you might be feeling grief.

Now that we have an idea of what is happening inside you, it is time to risk experiencing the actual discomfort of the loss. You might be yelling *no*, but remember what we talked about earlier. The way out of this pain is to let yourself feel, without condemnation, what you may have been pushing away for a very long time.

During this journey, you may say to yourself, *It seems all I do is experience this pain*. We are addressing that now. Belief it or not, by looking at your sorrow in full, by allowing yourself to completely experience it, you loosen its hold on you.

The way we feel after a loss is different for everyone. There is no magic formula. However, I ask people to spend a little time each day remembering their hurt as they work through grief. It is crucial to permit yourself to be sad.

However, just as importantly, after you have allowed yourself to experience the feelings associated with your loss, it is also essential that you do not stay in this place. Active, healthy grieving requires balance. You do this by matching the time you spend directly working on your wounds with the time you spend coping with your day-to-day life. Give yourself space to cry, yell, or whatever it takes, but after a set time, tell those emotions to meet you the next day so you can move forward, grow, and learn from your journey.

For example, set an alarm that goes off at 5 p.m. each day. At that hour, set a timer for thirty minutes. During this half hour, go through your memories and sadness surrounding your grief. Allow it to happen. If it feels out of control, arrange for safe person to be with you, or schedule this on a regular basis with a counselor. When the timer goes off, tell those emotions you will return to them tomorrow. If they pop up during the day, remind them that you haven't forgotten them and you will attend to them at 5 p.m. Do the same thing the following day, and continue until you feel the sadness or sorrow begin to lighten.

Reframe the Event

Sometimes our grief is easy to pinpoint, like when we've lost a friend or a family member. Other times, it is harder to understand. It may be difficult to grasp the depth of a partner's betrayal or an unexpected job displacement. In those cases, we may need to spend time searching for understanding and maybe even reframing our hurt. In other words, we need to somehow try to make emotional sense of what just occurred in our lives.

Once you realize how you feel about a disrupting situation, the next step will be discovering the need to possibly reframe the event. This will allow you to develop an understanding of what happened in order to move beyond it. Reframing is what happens when you ask yourself what you learned from the experience—about yourself, others, or the circumstance.

For example, if I were just fired from a job, I would possibly be angry at myself and my old boss. It would be helpful to take that moment to assess the conditions around the situation honestly. For instance, I would ask myself

- *Did I really enjoy that job?*
- *Did I have the skills necessary for the position?*
- *Was I clear on my understanding of the job? Did I have a true grasp of what my employer expected of me?*

Reframing the circumstances is about taking action that incorporates what you've learned in order to move forward toward the best outcome.

When you reframe a hurtful event like the one above, take time to think about and journal your responses as you ask yourself

- *How can I use this event to help navigate my future?*
- *Do I need more training? In what areas?*
- *Am I better suited to specific types of employers or bosses?*

Tie Up Loose Ends

After you have tried to name some of your feelings, taken time to experience them where necessary, and possibly reframed what really happened, then what? The next step in healing is to tie up any loose ends.

Is there anything you need to do or say to move on? Do you need to forgive yourself or someone else? Do you need to make amends? Many people spend time forgiving and letting go of the past during this stage. Take time to write out the action steps you may want to make to complete your restoration process.

Grief is often described as the process of healing from wounds. In a perfect world, injuries heal completely over time. However, there are times when our active cooperation is needed. Praying, receiving comfort, and talking to friends and God about your loss are ways of tending to your grief.

In the end, God will act as a compassionate Father by comforting our sorrow: "He will wipe every tear from their eyes. There will be no more death or mourning or crying or pain, for the old order of things has passed away" (Revelation 21:4 NIV). Until then, He calls us to come to Him with what is on our hearts, as seen in 1 Peter 5:7 (NIV), "Cast all your anxiety on him because he cares for you." The grieving process does not make the situation disappear or the hurt leave our lives. But it can help heal the feelings connected to those losses. In fact, our grief recovery can help us grow a bigger, healthier world around the injury or the wound.

What does it look like to grow a healthier world? Some people have said to think of your heartache as the pit of a peach. The situation that caused you pain is the pit. Your grief recovery or mended feelings are the fruit that grows around the pit. These mended or healed wounds are our new way of viewing the world. As we heal, we understand the hurt and the pain are still a part of us but do not consume us. Our recovery can help us grow into someone healthier, better equipped to handle losses in the future and to comfort others who are struggling.

Immediately after your loss, it feels like it almost consumes your life. You will have many firsts, and many ups and downs as time goes on. However, soon you might start reconnecting with your family and friends and have moments when you feel joyful and happy again. As these positive experiences accumulate, your grief remains a part of you, but it no longer dominates your daily thoughts and emotions. Your life has grown around the pain, making the pit smaller and less significant, but still a part of you.

The exercises below will help you master and gain positive experiences surrounding your grief. As you work through some of the activities, you will come to understand the phrase *reconciling with your grief*. We learn to understand our grief, and at the same time, we are forever changed by it.

Step 7 Exercises: Growing through Grief

1. Here is a list of reminders that others have found helpful in developing a self-care plan through their grieving process. Remember to treat yourself with the same empathy, tolerance, and affection you would extend to a valued friend in a similar situation.

   • Take whatever time you need to heal.

   • Pay attention to your eating, sleeping, and exercise patterns and routines.

   • Look for a counselor, support group, or safe friend to help you through the tough times.

   • Avoid taking on new responsibilities or making big decisions for a season.

   • Look for times to laugh and enjoy yourself during your healing.

   • Spend time daily to remember or feel your loss. As time goes on, your period of remembrance may evolve to a monthly interval.

   • Spend time in meditation and prayer.

   • Monitor yourself for signs of excessive sadness or hopelessness.

2. We all can struggle with adjustment and loss when it happens to us. We need to look inside ourselves during these seasons of grief and ask hard questions. Consider the following statements as examples, and journal any thoughts or regrets you may feel.

- *I wish I would have tried harder.*
- *I wish I could take back those words.*
- *I wish I could say I was sorry.*
- *I wish I could forget that ever happened.*
- *I wish I would have spent the time when I could.*

Our regrets and mistakes are not the whole story. When we reframe the event, we need to remind ourselves of what is in our control and what is not. Treat yourself with grace and compassion. For example, you may remind yourself that

- *I did the best I could.*
- *I was young and did not know what I do now.*
- *I have asked for forgiveness, and I am not responsible for the rest.*
- *With God's help, my memory will be free of fear.*
- *I cared for them with the resources I had at the time.*

3. Ask yourself the following questions and remember to write your responses down. Don't edit your thoughts. Dig deep and be honest with yourself. Your answers may change the storyline that keeps playing over and over in your memory.
- *If it was another person feeling regret and loss, what would I say to them?*
- *What two or three things do I need to remind myself of every day to keep moving forward with my healing?*

- *What people and situations need to be part of the healing and restoration plan toward my sound mind and joyful life?*

Remember your Revelation 21:4 promise.

4. Psychology and research have told us that memories are a permanent part of who we are.[1] This is excellent if your memories are good, but hard if they are not. When we deal with wounds, the reminders of the hurt and pain can sometimes be unbearable. While it is not possible to erase memories from your mind, there are strategies to change how a memory makes you feel. The simplest way to do this is to associate good things with bad impressions. The goal is to make these painful recollections less agonizing through positive association. New emotional experiences will start to change how those triggers make you feel.

    For example, do something that makes you happy while thinking about a bad memory. Let's say that I had a recollection where ugly words were said about me. At the time I was feeling sad, I could go for a run, call a friend, take a bubble bath, or listen to some good music. This exchange will allow me to begin to associate good feelings with painful ones. The next time I have a trigger of those mean words, my brain will remember both the good and the ugly. In time, my new memories will lessen the pain of the event and the bad memories.

Even though this concept might be easy to understand, it can be a little more difficult to put into practice. If you get stuck at any point along the way, please reach out to a friend or a professional for guidance and support.

Step 8: Access Joy in Your Relationships

> May the God of hope fill you with all joy and peace as you trust in him,
> so that you may overflow with hope by the power of the Holy Spirit.
>
> Romans 15:13 NIV

Sometimes when we feel challenged by life's problems, we may think it would be easier to give up and stay angry at the world. Joy is a powerful and essential emotion that plays a significant role in shaping our lives and overall well-being. It can uplift our spirits, improve our mental health, and enhance our overall quality of life.

Nehemiah 8:10 (NIV) tells us, "The joy of the LORD is your strength." It's important for us to understand what was happening in Nehemiah's time when he said this. The Israelites had just returned to Jerusalem from exile. They were listening to the Torah being read at the temple. As they listened, they were overcome with condemnation and began weeping because they felt they had let God down.

Nehemiah 8:10–12 (NLT) says:

"Go and celebrate with a feast of rich foods and sweet drinks and share gifts of food with people who have nothing prepared. This is a sacred day before our Lord. Don't be dejected and sad, for the joy of the LORD is your strength!"
And the Levites, too, quieted the people, telling them, "Hush! Don't weep! For this is a sacred day."

So the people went away to eat and drink at a festive meal, to share gifts of food, and to celebrate with great joy because they had heard God's words and understood them. Instead of continuing to push more shame at this downcast group, Nehemiah told them to go celebrate with a meal together. How cool is that?

However, joy—in its fuller, spiritual meaning of expressing God's goodness—involves much more than cheer and happiness with friends. This type of joy is a deep-rooted happiness that comes from being surrounded and consumed with Him. What does it mean to have this type of joy?

If you are like me, you may have had times when you were struggling to find that place of joy in your life, and you may have wondered:

- *What is really going on with me when I can't feel happy?*
- *Why can't I get out of this ditch?*
- *Why does everything feel so hard?*

Are you aware that your lack of joy can also make you less willing to be around people? Most of us don't want to be around others when we're not joyful. It makes perfect sense. That makes Nehemiah's actions even more intriguing.

Research tells us that when our relational pathways or joy centers are working, we are more likely to feel like interacting with people—we want to connect. We are relationally present in our friendships.[1]

As an emotional control center, our brain can be connected or disconnected depending on what is happening with our feelings at the time. Being joyful activates several areas of the brain (including the right frontal cortex, the precuneus, the left amygdala, and the left insula). When we experience feelings of joy, these areas connect and are activated. When we are joyful, we naturally feel close to others in our lives. The opposite is also true when our adverse reactions are in control.

For instance, say someone cuts you off in traffic, or your child talks back to you for the fifth time within the hour. You may get angry and say things that you don't mean. At this point, you are neither joyful nor feeling connected to the people in front of you. When our adverse reactions are in control, we can lose any flexibility with trying to understand our circumstances. We are not able to put ourselves in someone else's shoes. It isn't easy to see things from their perspective.

The relational part of our brain is offline.

Is it possible this is what was happening to the Israelites in the story of Nehemiah? They had been in exile. They had been away from God and were feeling disconnected. As a result, this caused them great sorrow. As a remedy for their sadness, they were told to have dinner together.

This act of community would help to ignite their relational pathways. One of the outcomes of this interaction is feelings of improved connection to each other and God. This action had the beneficial promise of bringing them joy and strength.

Both our brains and the book of Nehemiah are telling us that if we can learn to stay relational, we can increase the likelihood that we will go throughout our day in joyfulness. How cool is that!

When those confrontations with the boss or a friend or spouse come at us, being intentional about remaining connected to people will increase our joy factor. In this emotional state, we are more self-aware. We say and do things that align with who we were created to be. Ultimately, we are a much better version of ourselves.

When we understand how being relational and joy are connected, then we can appreciate the ability to feel and show joy doesn't come from the good or bad circumstances of our lives. It comes from our trust in or our intimate relationship with God. It settles in us when we know Him in our hearts, not just our heads. The Scriptures tell us we can't lose joy any more than we can lose God (see John 16:22). We are told that joy is a spiritual gift, and we can have it forever as we trust Him. Romans 15:13 (NIV) conveys joy as a gift that comes with trust: "May the God of hope fill you with all joy and peace as you trust in him."

How to Access Continual Joy

The story of Ruth and Naomi demonstrates the importance of knowing that we can access continual joy as we choose to trust God with our circumstances.

For those who have not read this story, here is an overview. Ruth is Naomi's daughter-in-law. Naomi, her husband, and two sons decide to move to Moab because there was a famine in their hometown of Bethlehem. While there, Naomi's husband tragically dies. The boys get married to local girls, and about ten years later, both of her sons pass away. As was the custom, the daughters-in-law stayed with Naomi until she decided she wanted to return to her home in Bethlehem. At that time, Naomi tells them to return to their fathers' households in Moab so they can potentially get married again. However, Ruth, one of the daughters-in-law, chooses instead to go to Bethlehem with Naomi. She tells her decisively, "Where you go, I will go. . . . Your people shall be my people, and your God, my God" (Ruth 1:16 NASB).

As Naomi and Ruth arrive in Bethlehem, the local women recognize and call Naomi by name. Naomi responds to their greetings by telling them to call her Mara instead of Naomi. The name *Mara* means "bitterness." I am guessing you and I would feel the same. Whether these women actually call her Mara is unknown.

Why is the meaning significant? Just like each of us, her name was her identity. Her given name, *Naomi*, means "to be pleasant, sweet, delightful, beautiful."[2] In Greek, the word for joy is *chara*. The words *Naomi* and *chara* have similar meanings. Both denote a feeling of inner gladness, delight, or rejoicing. Naomi was destined to be a person who carried joy. However, the things happening at this point sure didn't line up with that promise. It is a powerful story that I encourage you to read if you haven't. Ruth's trust and willingness to stay in a relationship with both her mother-in-law and God caused her to succeed greatly in love and life.

Happiness can elude us if it is based on the circumstances of our current events. In fact, sometimes, I am not ecstatic with what is going on in my everyday events. However, true joy is always within our reach, no matter what happens. We all have the power to ask for godly gladness, regardless of our situations.

Steps to Staying Joyful

Let's look at a couple of ways to stay in that place of joy in our daily lives.

1. Ask in Jesus' name. John 16:24 tells us:

Until now you've not been bold enough to ask the Father for a single thing in my name, but now you can ask, and keep on asking him! And you can be sure that you'll receive what you ask for, and your joy will have no limits!

Jesus is saying when you ask for something in Jesus' name, in some way, your prayer will be answered. When this action is taken from a place of dependence on God, you will receive an answer.

Let's be clear, asking for a million dollars in your bank account is not what the verse is talking about here. The focus is on praying about and believing God—which includes believing and sometimes waiting for Him to heal emotions, restore relationships, or send essential provisions that will bring you peace and joy.

What this verse is saying matters to our joy factor.

If you continue to sow into your relationship with God, you have the promise your joy will have no limits. Prayer (talking to God) and meditation (listening to God) helps your brain stay in relationship mode. Spend some time being bold enough to ask God to replace the things that are keeping you from feeling freedom in your joy.

Do you need a new job?

Do you need to improve a damaged relationship?

Do you need a fresh start?

Work at finding ways of communicating with God that help you notice and enjoy more of His daily presence.

2. Find humor in all things. It may sound weird, but another way to increase your joy is to look for ways to improve your sense of humor and appreciate the people in your world. This task might sound too simple, but let's examine the evidence.

Isha Gupta, a neurologist from IGEA Brain and Spine, tells us a smile spurs a chemical reaction in the brain, releasing certain hormones, including dopamine and serotonin.[3] Dopamine increases our feelings of happiness. Serotonin is the hormone released and associated with reduced stress.

Patients in one study were asked to watch or read materials that made them smile or brought them happiness in some way. What this research found was conclusive proof that a good sense of humor can help people genuinely recover from illnesses and depression.[4]

Joy produces chemicals in our bodies that can support our immune systems, which can trigger both emotional and physical healing. The act of laughing has other long-term benefits.[5] It can relieve discomfort by causing the body to produce its own natural painkillers. The Bible confirms this in Proverbs 17:22, "A joyful, cheerful heart brings healing to both body and soul."

A good sense of humor can soothe pressure by teaching your body to relax. When it comes to tension, both laughing and smiling can cool down your anxiety responses. If you are one of many people who needs more laughter in your life, try a couple of the following:

- Look for a few pictures or videos that make you laugh and put them where you can see them regularly.
- Learn a couple of jokes to share with a friend or co-worker. Make sure that your jokes aren't hurtful.
- Reminisce with friends or family about things from your childhood that were funny and laugh together.
- Learn to laugh at goofy things you've done. For example, have you ever put salt instead of sugar on your cereal? Or have you brushed your teeth with something other than toothpaste, like baby ointment? (Okay, now you can laugh at me because I've done that! Yes, it tasted really, really bad.)

3. Another step to support joy is to help our brains sustain it by creating positive experiences. When we meet with people who are happy to see us, or when we have the satisfaction of creating something beautiful, we are instilling positive experiences that condition our brains to sustain joy. With these simple acts, we are diminishing the anxious feelings and thoughts in the noisy back of the brain.

Decide Who Is Really in Charge

Jorge came to see me to talk about his wife. She was struggling with their marriage and wanted out of the relationship. According to him, they had already gone through a lot together. They had experienced great times—with phenomenal jobs, the birth of babies, and building new houses. And, there were also some not-so-good times when they lost loved ones too soon and suffered under the pressure of addictions. He said they had fought to be a healthy couple since the beginning of their marriage, but they could not connect. However, this drastic move by his wife surprised him. For months he tried everything he could to bring this woman back to their home. He ran the gamut of asking, threatening, guilting, and finally manipulating. None of it changed her mind, and he was miserable and depressed.

With nowhere else to turn, he decided to lean into God for help. This has also been my last choice at times, and I would recommend going to Him much earlier in your hurt. Jorge began to spend time walking and talking with Him. His situation did not change over the next several months, but he did. He became calm in the midst of the mess and chaos. He pressed into the Lord for His strength, and walked in true peace, love, and *complete joy*. If you had met him, you would never have known the daily stress he was experiencing. He had given up his hyper-control and was content being loved and supported in the process.

What Jorge did required courage and discipline. When we stop trying to control our lives and let God undertake things on our behalf, we will look differently at the circumstances that trouble us. Nothing destroys joy faster than trying to make things happen *for* God. I know this can be a struggle for many of us. If you are lacking this confidence, ask Him to help you trust more. Remember, being more relational with God and others will increase your joy and your peace.

In our story in the Song of Songs, the King is head over heels in love with His bride, and she is learning to depend on and trust Him. The Jerusalem maidens tell her:

> What love is this? How could you continue to care so deeply for him? Isn't there another who could steal away your heart? We see now your beauty, more beautiful than all the others. What makes your beloved better than any other?
>
> Song of Songs 5:9

At this point, her friends are trying to understand how she got to the place where she was so enamored, so hopeful, and so filled with joy. They can't figure out how, with all the ups and downs in this romance, she can love her groom so deeply.

Like Jorge, the Shulamite bride had been through a time of testing. However, her faith and reliance in someone they couldn't see, had grown rather than wavered. Her friends who watched her love story unfold became transfixed by her dedication and strength in the highs and lows. In the same way, I was impressed with Jorge.

My own journey toward joy was similar. I had to walk toward trust again. Even when it did not make sense to my brain, my spirit and emotions desired to feel happy and content again. There were times when I purposely engaged in activities in my pursuit of joy. I remember throwing a small party at our house after one of the kid's football games. It surprised everyone when I volunteered, but it did wonders for my mind and emotions. Or, there was a time the children and I sat down to have a serious talk about the holidays. One of the boys told a joke, then someone laughed, and pretty soon we were all smiling at a time that could have been very somber.

I also had to place boundaries around my thoughts; I didn't allow them to land automatically. I would purposely change the channel when I started reminiscing about hurts or betrayals. I made sure I was prepared with replacement thoughts and Scriptures that would bring me joy.

Joy is a fundamental aspect of the human experience that enriches our lives in countless ways. It's not just a fleeting emotion, but a profound state of being that has the potential to transform our lives and the world around us.

Step 8 Exercises: Intentional Joy

1. For us to have amazing relationships, we have to want them, plan for them, and at times, work for them. Having good partners and friends can buffer or lesson our stress responses, which is likely one reason why positive relationships are great for our health. Try these exercises to help refocus your emotions, stay in relationship, and sustain joy.

   • Write down the top five ways you know you are in relational mode. What does that feel or look like for you? Do you feel a little lighter, smile more, want to be with people? Maybe you even desire to send those texts with all the heart emojis. Those are the days you want to schedule coffee with a friend rather than shut off the phone.

   • Next, list five activities that positively affect your desire to be relational. Often this is time spent doing things we enjoy. For example, do you like taking a bubble bath, walking on the beach, reading a good book, or watching a movie? Set aside time to practice doing at least one of these daily. We need to remember these are our targets if joy is our end goal.

   • Now, make a list of the top five triggers that make you step away from being relational. Some things may include fighting with someone, being overtired, or even being hungry.

   • Then, plan what you will do when—not *if*—one of these things happens. How will you avoid pulling

back from people? Write these actions items down
and post them somewhere, or, if you're really brave,
share them with a friend. Most importantly, practice them as often as you can.

2. To help your brain release more dopamine, list ten
things that make you smile. Get creative. Maybe just
making people laugh at a goofy face works for you.
Practice at least one of these every day and track
your mood. Do you feel lighter and maybe even a bit
more joyful?

Proverbs 15:15 says it well: "Everything seems to
go wrong when you feel weak and depressed. But
when you choose to be cheerful, every day will bring
you more and more joy and fullness."

3. Think about some people in your life who you know
are crazy joyful. Are they also relational?

What things do you think they do to get themselves into that position in life? Are they more intentional about connecting? Do they show appreciation
for life? Do they take time to calm their minds, emotions, and spirits? If you aren't sure, consider sending
them a text and asking.

If you are not feeling all the joy you want in your
life, try practicing some of the things you admire in
the joyful people you identified. See if it changes how
you connect with others and with God.

Step 9: Who Are You Listening To?

Trust in the Lord completely, and do not rely on your own opinions. With all your heart rely on him to guide you, and he will lead you in every decision you make. Become intimate with him in whatever you do, and he will lead you wherever you go.

Proverbs 3:5–6

These verses offer a lot of guidance when answering the big question of who we should listen to in our lives. They capture one of the most crucial instructions on internal peace and love: any individual who wants to succeed in life should include and rely on God. We aren't told to listen to and lean into peer pressure, people on social media, news outlets, or the latest trends, but to trust in God and rely on His thoughts. Talk about straightforward, plain, and simple!

So, who are you listening to?

As we work toward understanding our real selves, this is an important question that needs to be addressed. If you want true success and sincere guidance that won't steer you wrong, you will need to consider whose direction you heed on life's journey. We would ask you to reflect on the idea of what you need to do if the voices speaking into you are causing you more stress than peace. This verse tells us we are never alone on the path of life. When we build a daily relationship with Someone who knows us inside and out, we experience comfort, order, and love. And the best part is that this same Creator *wants* to walk with us every step of the way, through the good times and the chaos.

The day our middle child was born is a good example of leaning on God's peace during the traumatic unknown. I remember it like it was yesterday. We were finishing a pretty average nine-month pregnancy and were expecting the same with our labor and delivery. Our obstetrician happened to be a good friend and neighbor, so the whole hospital encounter felt a little more relaxed.

At one point, it seemed not much was happening with the birthing progress, so my husband and my doctor decided they would go have dinner. I had been given an epidural, so I was not in pain. But in my gut, I knew something wasn't right with their plan. I now know that was the Holy Spirit talking to me. I remember telling myself, *You are in a hospital, for heaven's sake, there will be someone to help if you need it. Stop being so fearful.* So instead of demanding they stay, I just asked my doctor to ensure things were okay with the baby and me before they left. She reminded me that just fifteen minutes ago, I was only dilated four to five centimeters, and there was no need for concern. My gut feeling again told me to insist, so she relented and checked. And discovered that I was already at ten centimeters—apparently, Zach was in a hurry! It was time to get into birthing mode.

Within seconds, the room came alive with nurses, carts, and gowns. Minutes later, Zach arrived. He was a big baby and immediately had everyone's attention, but not in a good way. He was not breathing.

Both my husband and I watched in horror as the doctors and nurses worked on our newborn son. Minute after minute, there was no sound, no cry, no breath from our baby.

At one point, my doctor friend tried to attend to me, and I remember getting very angry, telling her to make Zach breathe! In desperation, Neal and I cried out to God, "Please fix this—please make him breathe and let him live!"

Do you know what I heard at that moment? Absolutely nothing. Hearing nothing is not what you want to experience when you really need an immediate answer. However, what I felt in my spirit was immediate and complete calm. My body relaxed, and I was quiet inside. It seemed more logical that I would have continued to panic and yell orders to everyone. But instead, I felt peace. You know, the type of peace that passes all understanding? That's exactly what I felt. I knew, without a shadow of a doubt, that everything was going to be okay.

Did I know what would happen to Zach? No. But I did know that my prayers had been heard, and God had the outcome covered. This type of tranquility offers us deep, abiding encouragement, strength, comfort, value, and acceptance. When we call out to Him, God gives us an understanding that does not make sense to us in the current situation of our lives.

A few minutes later, there was a joyous sound. Zach yelled. And then yelled some more. Many weeks later, medical professionals warned us of the dangers of Zach not breathing for that long. I remember the conversation well. They had to tell me the potential risks. But oddly, I did not hear much of what they said. I simply could not comprehend that it would not turn out okay. Maybe I was being naïve, but when their words hit me, so did that feeling of quiet and calm. I knew I was hearing their words of warning, but I was also remembering the scene from the hospital. You may understand what I mean when I say that moment runs in slow motion in my mind. And so does the strength I felt from the instant connection with God over the situation. That peace is like being in a bad storm but not afraid of the waves. I can dial that up when I remember the room that day. Honestly, I will use that experience whenever my peace gets really rocked. Every time, the memory takes me to a place of knowing Someone a lot bigger than me has got this, and it is good!

As it turned out, Zach was a wonderful baby who was very normal and healthy. I know God was teaching me how to listen for His voice of peace when I was full of fear and confusion. He was trying to teach me to be confident in hearing Him and following His peace more than fear.

Find Peace in the Midst of Chaos

You and I know there are a lot of voices we *could* choose to listen to. We need to weed through them to find the one speaking peace. To get through each day, every hurdle and obstacle that comes our way, we need to be looking to lay hold of God's voice, His peace. He promises to give it to us, but we must lean into it, believe it, and take hold of it before it will do us any good.

Here is one of those promises: "Peace I leave with you; my peace I give you. I do not give to you as the world gives. Do not let your hearts be troubled and do not be afraid" (John 14:27 NIV).

I remember when I was in my early thirties, I met an older gentleman who asked me to tell him my story. I thought to myself, *What story? What does he want to know?* So I said, "There is not much to tell, life has been pretty normal." He turned to me and said, "Just wait, you haven't lived long enough." If you are thinking, *Okay then, what an old crank*—so was I! What I didn't realize at the time was he was telling me that all life has its troubles. It's not that God hates you, or you haven't lived right. It's not karma. He was saying life is challenging. It just is.

The answer to those challenges is in John 14:27. Jesus promises to give us His peace, then He follows immediately with the instruction to not let our hearts be troubled. He is well aware of and understands the difficult things you and I come up against in our lives. We need peace because our hearts *will* experience trouble—every single one of us. This verse tells us that if we take hold of the promise of His peace, we can have calm, untroubled hearts, regardless of our external circumstances. Many of us get stuck because we have trouble grabbing on to the voice that brings peace to our lives—God's voice.

Let me challenge you to turn your situation around by learning how to lean into God's voice. This discipline involves patience, practice, and faith. We can learn to discern His voice amidst the noise and voices of the world.

Let Go of Your Past—Embrace the Truth

Have you noticed many things in life just don't make sense? Do you feel there is a lot that is beyond your control? What do you do in those situations? Panic? Go numb? Jump into action any way you can?

Research tells us that apprehension and turmoil are seldom focused on our present-day circumstances.[1] Normally, it is trouble borrowed from either the past or the future. Some people worry about things that might happen. Others get stressed about things that have already happened and they wish they could change. A third category hops between the two. I know, I have camped there now and then.

Colossians 3:15 (AMPC) compares Christ's peace to that of an umpire.

> Let the peace (soul harmony which comes) from Christ rule (act as umpire continually) in your hearts [deciding and settling with finality all questions that arise in your minds, in that peaceful state] to which as [members of Christ's] one body you were also called [to live]. And be thankful (appreciative), [giving praise to God always].

What does an umpire do? They make real-time game decisions. We are to depend so much on the peace of Christ that it becomes a guide, or an umpire, to help us make life choices.

But what is the truth about all of life's troubles? Bottom line: both the future *and* the past are under the care of God. More importantly, they are not where you and I live. We only exist in the present. As far as the future goes, God promises to supply your future needs. And it may blow your mind, but God has chosen to rewrite the heavenly consequences of your past—if you ask Him to.

We are all guilty of trying to take control in some way, right? I don't know about you, but I do it all the time. It is so easy to waste a lot of time and energy trying to figure things out, and then try to put ourselves into the plan to make them work. Well, the good news is that we can stop wasting our time and energy, because we can choose to let this "heavenly umpire" or guide have our back.

People have told me on more than a few occasions when they finally stopped trying to figure out why God allowed something to happen and just started trusting, a weird calm came to them. Much like me in the hospital with my son, this enables us to face the fact that not all of our questions are going to be answered in this lifetime. Trusting in His plan and listening to His voice can bring us peace.

Moving from Control to Letting Go

My friend Sandy recently came out of a love-hate relationship with her young adult son, Erik. She spent most of his teenage years tracking him. She knew where he was and what he was up to via his phone, friends, or car. Yes, she even tracked his car.

When she did this, how do you think Erik responded? You guessed it. Horribly. In fact, things kept getting worse in their communication and relationship until one day Sandy realized that she was losing a bunch of battles with this game. Her connection with her son was severely damaged; she was exhausted and just couldn't do it anymore. If she stopped the hyper managing, she feared the worst for her child but realized she needed to end all the spying and controlling. So, one day, she gave up. Disconnected all the devices and decided to trust God with her son.

So, what happened to Erik? At first, he loved his new-found freedom and continued down some self-destructive paths. He found friends who partied rather than worked, he dropped out of his band because no one was reminding him to practice, and his friendships plummeted because he didn't like to return texts. Like most of our bad habits, his caught up to him with a bang.

But luckily for him, he woke up to reality and decided to make some tough life choices. He learned he needed to eat, and in order to do that, he needed to go to work consistently. He also learned that he needed to establish appropriate boundaries with his friends and his time.

Today, Erik is succeeding in life, and Sandy is at peace. Why? She decided to live in the present and took the leap of trust in her life.

Understanding, listening for, and applying God's peace like an umpire is what brings order to chaos. It may be a different journey for each of us. However, if you want to walk in true peace—where you know all will be well with you and your plans—then listening for and knowing this voice is necessary. Instead of rejection, fear, shame, and hopelessness, you can have internal calm. Try some of the following exercises to practice hearing the right voice in your life.

Step 9 Exercises: Know the Right Voice

1. Work to remind yourself about the difference between truths—in the moment, is it yours or God's?

    Take a moment to filter your thoughts through these four questions:

    • Does what you believe in the moment bring you peace?

    • Does what you believe in the moment borrow from the past or the future?

    • Does what you believe in the moment tear you down or lift you up?

    • Does what you believe line up with God's truths?

Since the Bible is filled to overflowing with beautiful insights, sometimes it helps to focus on just a few key verses when we need to figure out if we are hanging on to our own truths or His.

    Here are two passages to help you in that process of exchange and in recognizing the right Spirit.

> Finally, brothers and sisters, whatever is true, whatever is noble, whatever is right, whatever is pure, whatever is lovely, whatever is admirable—if anything is excellent or praiseworthy—think about such things.
>
> Philippians 4:8 NIV

But the fruit of the Spirit is love, joy, peace, forbearance, kindness, goodness, faithfulness, gentleness and self-control.

Galatians 5:22–23 NIV

2. Take time to read Song of Songs (I recommend reading it from The Passion Translation). Pay special attention to chapter 7, verses 4–5, which says:

Such discernment surrounds you, protecting you from the enemy's advance. Redeeming love crowns you as royalty. Your thoughts are full of life, wisdom, and virtue. Even a king is held captive by your beauty.

Now answer these questions about the story:

- How is the bride protected?
- How does the bridegroom describe her?
- Can you try to pretend someone loves and appreciates you as much as the bridegroom does in these verses? (Don't worry about whether you are a bride or a bridegroom—can you speak those affirming words over yourself?)
- Has anyone ever talked with you like that? This is God's truth over His bride—you and me. How does that feel to hear?
- Can you let the truth of the present thoughts and words into your heart? If your answer to this is still no, let's continue to work on this together through these exercises.

Sometimes the words that we remember are hurtful or painful. Often they are from the past. Even if your hurtful words are in the present, *choose* what is truth, and it will give you peace. These terms of endearment and affection in Song of Songs describe an endless love we cannot push or chase away.

Choose to believe the fact that His nature for you is love. In Song of Songs 1:15, the bridegroom tells the Shulamite woman, "My darling, you are so lovely! You are beauty itself to me. Your passionate eyes are like gentle doves."

If the God who made the universe speaks these things over you, why are you not celebrating that you are loved, special, and very distinct? Many of us have a hard time believing God's incredible love for us. Even if we don't believe or understand it yet, we need to settle the fact that it is truth. No matter how rough your road in life has been, you *are* loved, and you matter. Because God's nature is love. Friends, let that one sink in!

3. This week, work to increase your ability to listen to a supportive voice. To do this, consider using a counseling technique called *grounding*. Grounding is a way of focusing with a purpose of pulling us back on track. It is designed to anchor us in the present moment, pulling us away from future worry or anxious thoughts. It is a skill to use when you are having a bad day or dealing with a lot of stress. Grounding helps reorient you to the here-and-now.

If I connect or ground with what's happening in the world or culture, then I will look to the world to determine my well-being. If I ground with or focus on things of the Spirit of God, I will look to Him as my guide for stability and peace.

You can ground in the Spirit by focusing on some aspect of God's truth. Where do people find this truth?

- Some people will choose to listen to calming or worship music.
- Some will read Bible verses that touch their hearts.
- Others will pray or read material from teachers who reorient them to the present or the truth.

No matter what you choose, make sure you make a good space to work on this exercise. Go somewhere where you are not distracted by internal thoughts and outside feelings that are causing you distress. If you love nature, go to a park. If you like to be pampered, take a bath. If you enjoy exercise, take a walk or run. Use your imagination.

Step 10: Practice the Discipline of Peace

There is no fear in love. But perfect love drives out fear, because fear has to do with punishment. The one who fears is not made perfect in love.

1 John 4:18 NIV

In a previous chapter, I talked about my husband being diagnosed with stage four cancer at thirty-eight years old. I can easily say that this was one of the scariest moments of my life. If you have ever been in a place where you have no power and considerable ambiguity, then you understand. You quickly realize how little control you have. We were thankful that during this long and difficult process, we had amazing friends, excellent doctors, an incredible support system, and a patient God.

I still remember the look on the doctor's face when he told us that he had found a mass on Neal's colon. Friends, you know it's serious when the doctor tells you he would like to schedule the surgery for the next day. Within hours, we were talking to hospital staff and cancer care. I can't remember how many inches they took out of him, but it was a lot. Those hours were grueling as we waited. It was harrowing to know there were a handful of people desperately working to prolong my husband's life in another part of the hospital. They would take a section of his colon, freeze it, and have it analyzed. They kept going until they found a section that was not infected. This process took close to six hours, was dangerous, and changed the course of his recovery. We didn't find out until later how diligent the surgeon was in getting to the source of the problem.

Because they worked so hard to ensure they removed all the cancer cells, the operation was tougher on his body. His internal systems were stressed, and his colon strained to get back to processing food normally. Neal ended up being in the hospital for close to two extra weeks.

Every day I would go to the hospital to spend time with him while he healed. Then I would run home to care for three scared little boys. I remember one evening leaving the hospital exhausted, worried, and almost numb. I found my car in the pouring rain and started driving from downtown to our home. I began to sob and ask God what we were supposed to do next. More specifically, where was He right then? Why did it feel like He was not answering my prayers? On this particular day, I was frustrated at everything, especially at the injustice of it all. My disappointment was also directed at God. As I was rolling down the highway, I started telling the Lord what I thought of the situation.

I remember looking out my window at the people in the vehicles next to me. I'm sure they thought I was crazy as I talked out loud with no one else in the car. I was telling God how unfair this whole mess was for our family. At one point, when I finally became quiet, the craziest thing happened. I heard a voice so clearly it was like someone was sitting next to me in my car.

I heard the words, "I love you."

Now, what do you do with that? Well, what *I* did was I said, "I don't understand, and I need more right now. I need some help with this disease, and I need some answers."

Perfect Love Casts Out Fear

The Lord was telling me what I could not comprehend at the time: perfect love casts out fear, as we see in 1 John 4:18 above.

Understandably, at this time in my life I was fearful. I know now that God did not want me to carry that fear. At some level, we all understand that, but what I was going through was really scary. And maybe you have had a similar experience.

The lesson that started in my car that day ended up being a long journey of trying to understand how to replace my fear with His peace.

It is easy to see there is much more fear and stress in this world than peace and acceptance. Isn't it ironic that given today's communication technology—which is more significant than it has ever been in the history of mankind—there has never been more misunderstanding and loneliness?

In place of peace, you may feel

- Discontentment because you aren't happy with yourself.

- Jealousy, because you are constantly comparing yourself to others.
- Fear and doubt because you lack trust.

All of these things together lead to an anguished soul that never succeeds in finding contentment, no matter how many friends you know, likes you receive, or stuff you have around you.

In my own rough journey, I learned God feels nothing but perfect love when He thinks of us. I don't know about you, but that was not the picture I got in Sunday school. I came through my grade school years with the understanding that we should not mess with God.

Over time, I discovered that God has a love-based identity for us. First Corinthians 13:5 confirms that by telling us that love "thinks no evil" (NKJV).

By God's own nature, He cannot think evil about you or me. Why? Because He is perfect love. Wow. (Sit with that for a minute.)

So, God's love flowing through us makes fear leave us. And then this same perfect love allows peace to surround our lives and our circumstances.

We could all use more of that, right?

The bridegroom explains the king's ultimate love and covenant relationship with her in Song of Songs 6:8–9:

I could have chosen any from among the vast multitude of royal ones who follow me. But unique is my beloved dove— unrivaled in beauty, without equal, beyond compare, the perfect one, the favorite one. Others see your beauty and sing of your joy. Brides and queens chant your praise: "How blessed is she!"

God knows you will struggle with trials and temptations, and sometimes fall, but you need to understand He still sees you as pure and lovely. His perfect love is not up for negotiation in our lives. It is ours for the taking!

Exchanging Fear for Abiding Peace

So, what are you afraid of? Not measuring up? Being, acting, and thinking differently than someone else? If you hold on to what God says about who you are, you will learn to rest in His love and embrace your own uniqueness.

What is really important is this can be done at the same time you let others accept *their* own destinies. When you focus on His promises for you, there is no need to measure yourself against the world's standard or anyone else. You will listen to His voice as your *own* drummer. That is what He was trying to tell me in the car that day, and as I hid in the closet after being betrayed, and so many other times in my life. His promise of perfect love was persistently trying to rid me of my fear.

God's tranquility gives you the ability to be yourself and know who you were created to be, even when the world would like you to be different. This kind of peace brings the understanding that even in the midst of difficulties, you will not go through them alone. Mary, the mother of Jesus, had to feel this peace in order to walk through God's plan for her life. Mary was minding her own business, when an angel showed up and told her she was pregnant without ever having sex. And, oh, by the way, the baby was the Son of God. Whoa!

Luke 1:38 gives us her reaction: "Mary responded, saying, 'Yes! I will be a mother for the Lord! As his servant, I accept whatever he has for me. May everything you have told me come to pass.'"

Imagine yourself in Mary's situation. You're moving through your day when an angel shows up and says you are chosen and honored among women because you'll give birth to God's Son. Your prize for that honor? You'll be unwed and pregnant during a time when that behavior is despised and could be punished by stoning (see Deuteronomy 22).

Most of us would be suspicious and probably freak out. We likely would not say, "Okay, I accept whatever my lot is in this life."

The only way Mary could have felt calm about the situation, while possibly simultaneously being afraid, was if she knew deep inside that she could trust the angel, and she could trust the calm she felt in her spirit. She knew God was with her. One of the hallmarks of God's presence is His peace, with its power to protect your heart and mind from worry and anxiety.

In Greek, the word *peace* means "to obtain quietness by removing what seeks to distract and destroy you."[1] It is an aggressive removal or a forceful extraction. A forceful extraction of what? Of anything that tries to destroy your inner quiet.

God's peace has a very similar meaning in the Old Testament. When we study the Hebrew pictographs, we find the word for "peace" does not merely mean a state of mind. It means to destroy or remove the chaos and anarchy around you.[2] Teacher John Paul Jackson tells us that when anxiety is removed, purpose emerges.

Based on this understanding, when Jesus said, "Peace be with you," He was not simply greeting people. No, He was issuing a command to the disarray surrounding their lives. Essentially, He was saying, "May the chaos and anarchy that is trying to keep you from a place of stillness be removed from your life." I think we all could use a little of that right now.

God's peace is not passive. It needs to be our standard for dealing with life's hopelessness and fear.

The Discipline of Peace

If we are honest, we all want the type of inner rest that Mary experienced—a place where she leaned in and trusted that all would be well in her life. Here are some disciplines that will bring you closer to that goal.

Discipline 1: Decide that peace is more important than understanding. If you have a problem or a decision to make, the peace of God is available to you whenever and wherever you are.

I once worked with a lady whose favorite activity was writing her life plan for the next five years. She did this "soothing activity" a day, a month, a year at a time. This behavior was due to her (false) belief that an orderly life on the outside would bring direction to her life on the inside, especially to her heart.

The Bible teaches us that God desires us to walk with Him, depending on His daily provisions and guidance, not to run out into the future without Him. That is not how He designed us. It is beyond our capacity.

You won't find peace by engaging in excessive planning and doing. It is not the path to lasting peace for your mind and spirit.

The peace that comes from God is timeless because He has already seen your future. He knows what is going to happen. He knows the good, the bad, and the ugly before they occur. Please understand, He does not send the bad. He did, however, craft your mind to continually communicate with Him through your words, thoughts, and actions in all circumstances. This gift is yours in both wonderful seasons and challenging times.

You and I need to be resolute in looking for His peace more than for perfect answers or solutions.

Discipline 2: Choose what you will focus on: your problems or the promised peace from God. Even when things don't make sense, we must learn to trust that God's purpose for us is good, and *choose* to trust.

Remember Proverbs 3:5–6 from Step 9? Verse 5 is worth repeating: "Trust in the Lord completely, and do not rely on your own opinions. With all your heart rely on him to guide you, and he will lead you in every decision you make." Through all the striving, God is urging us to simply trust Him.

You and I must face the fact that not all of our questions will be answered in this lifetime. Because the peace of God is not based on circumstances, like the world's peace, it may not make sense to our minds. Understanding is not a prerequisite to feeling His gentle calm in our spirits. In fact, needing to understand can sometimes get in the way of trust. Focus on that promised peace.

The Hebrew term *shalom* is roughly translated as the word *peace*. In Scripture, shalom means more than a state of mind or a state of being. Shalom means to be filled with peace and feel complete. When you are consumed with this state of peace and completeness, you will naturally start to feel good about yourself and your circumstances. You can stand a little straighter because you know deep inside that you have value. You are important. It is here your insecurities and bad self-talk begin to fade. You begin to feel and offer more shalom to yourself and others.

Discipline 3: If you want God's peace, you must actively seek it out in all circumstances. Just understanding this type of peace exists is not enough. Just training your mind to think differently will only get you partway there. But, Diane, just asking for peace sounds too simple. But let's look at this together. In Philippians 4:6–7, the apostle Paul says:

> Don't be pulled in different directions or worried about a thing. Be saturated in prayer throughout each day, offering your faith-filled requests before God with overflowing gratitude. Tell him every detail of your life, then God's wonderful peace that transcends human understanding, will guard your heart and mind through Jesus Christ.

Notice the order Paul teaches us to achieve this. He starts by saying how often we should be praying—continually. Then he instructs to offer faith-filled requests, with gratitude. Next, give God all the details of our lives. Unload our cares on Him. *Then* we will experience God's peace.

So according to Paul's instruction, thankful requests, followed by pouring out your heart to Him, will bring you peace. It looks like there is a cause-and-effect relationship here.

Prayer is the cause. Peace is the effect.

Now let's look at the word *guard*. Remember from chapter 9, the way it is used in this verse does not mean to keep imprisoned. It is used in a military sense, meaning to stand at a post and guard against the aggression of an enemy. What this is telling us is amazing: when God's peace is guarding your life, you have entered a secure place of protection.

How life-changing to know the peace of God stands guard to keep worry and insecurity from your heart. And prayer, filled with thanks and honest communication, is what brings us to this place of peace.

As you read and practice these disciplines, I pray you find God's peace in great and mighty ways.

Step 10 Exercises: Purposely Practice Peace

1. Practice being mindful of your thoughts and emotions. Mindfulness is a mental health therapy technique that promotes staying aware of your surroundings, thoughts, and spirit to be at peace.

   Mindfulness isn't a strange, mystical concept. The opposite of mindfulness could be portrayed as letting your emotions and negative thoughts run wild over your life. This is similar to being mindless and can be described as the quality of something having no meaning.

   Mindfulness is being intentional and living in the present moment. When you focus on the negative past or the worrisome future, you can end up with feelings of anxiety or despair. Mindfulness helps you notice life's goodness rather than focusing on negative circumstances, people, or events.

   To gauge your level of mindfulness, ask yourself these questions:

   • Am I attentive to the people who are in my life at this moment?

   • Do I work to stay in the moment and not borrow problems from the past or future?

   • Do I consider what my spirit tells me about the situation or relationship?

   • Do I stay attentive of the fact that I have a destiny in this life?

Make it a point to pursue peace and live in the moment. Pay attention to what is happening to your emotions as you take in what is going on around you. Is someone talking to you? Are the kids playing in the background? Is your phone dinging? How do your surroundings make you feel right now—tense and rushed, or calm?

Tell yourself you will use all your senses to stay open to what is happening around you and not try to fix or change it. Work to find joy in simple pleasures, like the kids' laughter, the smile of a friend, or the peace of quietness.

2. Find peace each day. Find a quiet place to think, reflect, and possibly write in a journal. While you are there, ask yourself: What do I need peace for today?

   Dig deeper by thinking about these questions:

   • *Do I feel unworthy or guilty?*
   • *Am I worried and feeling out of control?*
   • *Do I need help trusting God or even someone else?*
   • *Do I need support in an important situation?*

   Turn those concerns and issues over to God. Literally say, "God, I give these things to You. I cannot do it without Your help. Allow me to experience Your peace in these situations." Do yourself a favor and be patient with this process. Spend time listening for answers.

3. Remember God's peace. Search your memory for a time when you really felt God's peace over a situation or a person in your life. Maybe it was like my experience with Zach's birth, when I couldn't explain how or why, but my body, mind, and spirit calmed at knowing God was in control of the situation. If you can't think of one, ask God to show you one from your past or let you experience one now.

   After you have a memory in mind, reflect on these questions:

   • What did you feel or think about the event that was different from other times when you didn't encounter peace?
   • Where did you see or not see God in that situation?
   • What verses or phrases would best describe this time for you?

Step 11: Stand Up to Adversity

"Have I not commanded you? Be strong and courageous. Do not be afraid; do not be discouraged, for the Lord your God will be with you wherever you go."

Joshua 1:9 NIV

Let's face it, change is hard, and healing is necessary—and both take courage to actually complete. In fact, most people struggle to achieve the results they desire. Why? Because, as many of us have realized, pain and perseverance aren't fun.

If you have discovered in the last few chapters that there are areas of your life that need strengthening or repairing, it may take some courage to change direction and get back on track. With the lofty goal of uncovering the real you, be aware that it will not be simple to put into practice the things we have discussed.

Throughout the years, I've trained myself to overcome the desire to cave under pressure when things get hard. I had to work on developing a strong mind, built on knowing and understanding the truth. It took several years and many more difficult situations before I could say to myself, *This is not the plan God has for my life because here is what His Word tells me.* Or even, *I need to pray for direction before I decide about this because my choices or the world's options aren't as good as His.*

When change is hard, people will often try to encourage you by giving you a pep talk, or repeating what they have been told in the past. For example, have you ever been instructed to "keep a stiff upper lip"? As a counselor, I've learned this isn't always the best guidance in a situation. What can often happen with that well-meaning advice is you will end up hiding your emotions in the face of adversity rather than knowing what you are really feeling. Or how about the statement, "Never let them see you sweat"? We know this isn't about a better deodorant choice. No, what people often mean is to pretend like you're in control even when things are falling apart. It means, at all costs, don't show your emotions. Can you relate to some of these comments that are meant to encourage us? Unfortunately, they fall short of giving us the courage needed in the moment.

In my struggle to avoid difficulties or experiences that I saw as unnecessary pain, I made a vow to stay in control and always be prepared. I came about this "stay organized and ahead of the game" mentality honestly. This gene was handed down to me through many generations. Both my mother and grandmother were always ready for any possible emergency on any given day. In fact, it was considered a weakness not to be.

As a young mother, I remember making emergency kits for all events. I would try to ensure we had "one of each" tucked away in the family van—extra water, spare Band-Aids, a couple of books for downtime, leftover makeup in case I was running late. I had a change of clothes for everyone and even a couple of tampons, just in case. I was trying my best to cover every base in order to ward off any problems that could possibly happen in life.

However, even with all this planning, an inevitable emergency came that I was unprepared for. It began when my son's assistant coach called to tell me he was worried the team wasn't ready for the next game. He added, "Your son is one of our leaders; if he shows up for practice today, others will as well." The problem was I knew better than to get on the roads that day because we had been given winter weather warnings.

What would you do in a situation like this? Are you one of those people who dare to stand their ground when they know what is right? Or are you like many of us who cave when people use persuasion?

I am better at it now, but on that particular day, I wasn't being brave. Don't get me wrong, listening to alternative points of view is good at times, but when you already know what you should be doing, why let well-meaning people or circumstances pull you off-course? That's all it took that day for me.

Even though deep in my unconscious I knew better, I took off with two children in tow in our "emergency-ready" van.

We got through the practice and were heading home. By then, it was snowing hard. We were close to entering our subdivision when the van hit a patch of ice and slid into a deep ditch. I tried as hard as possible to maneuver a way out, but the van was stuck fast. (It would have been helpful to have a shovel or some sand, but that wasn't in my emergency-ready kit.)

Never having experienced anything like this, we were all noticeably scared. After I worked to settle myself and my two younger boys down a little, I got out and walked around the van to assess the situation. Yep, there was no getting out, and it was getting dark. So, I did the only thing I could think to do. I got back into the driver's seat and panicked. I remember thinking that we would all be found in the morning—frozen. I could see the newspaper and email headlines in my mind: "Woman and Two Sons Found Frozen in Van." Worse, I realized that I was responsible because I knew we shouldn't have gone out. I was the preparedness queen, for crying out loud. I knew better.

I would like to tell you I had the courage of a warrior and immediately refocused on getting home safely. Instead, I think I played every possible horrible scenario in my head. I blamed myself for not having the emergency supplies to help us out. Looking back, I can now see I was not in real danger. I was within the city limits, and even though there were not a lot of people out on the road, there were emergency vehicles operating. However, I don't remember running any of those hopeful things through my mind. I just folded under the pressure of fear and self-condemnation.

In the end, someone with a much more snow-worthy vehicle found us and pulled our little troop out of the ditch. We were scared but not physically harmed by the adventure. It was a big lesson in seeing the need for patience and courage to listen to the right voice in making decisions.

Don't Cave Under Pressure

Nehemiah 8 tells the story of a similar problem on a much larger scale. Nehemiah was being coerced, distracted, and threatened to finish his assignment to build a wall around Jerusalem that would provide security and protection for the city. Up until this time, Nehemiah was in Babylon working for the king as a cupbearer.

The story opens with the news that those who had survived the exile were in great trouble and disgrace, with the walls of Jerusalem broken and its gates burned. Nehemiah pours out his heart to God, and asks for success before approaching the king for help. The king gave him everything he had the courage to ask for: a leave of absence to rebuild the wall, letters to ensure safety, and timber for the job. He even threw in an escort.

Under Nehemiah's leadership, the Jews withstood great opposition—including mocking and ridicule, physical threats, manipulation, and intimidation.

Something about his story made me think about how easily we tend to give in today, even when we know what makes sense. In my situation, I had a single-minded plan for making a coach happy. Even though I knew the safe thing to do was to stay home with my boys.

Nehemiah's goal was to remove the disgrace of Jerusalem, to rebuild the place God had chosen as a dwelling place for His name. Nehemiah's distractions and even betrayals during this process were most likely confusing and discouraging. But he had the courage and discipline to keep his eyes on the prize and remember his assignment.

In Nehemiah 6:2–4 (NIV), he tells us:

> Sanballat and Geshem sent me this message: "Come, let us meet together in one of the villages on the plain of Ono."
>
> But they were scheming to harm me; so I sent messengers to them with this reply: "I am carrying on a great project and cannot go down. Why should the work stop while I leave it and go down to you?" Four times they sent me the same message, and each time I gave them the same answer.

Things would have been much different if I'd had the courage to do what Nehemiah did in these verses. I was listening to thoughts that were derailing me from what I knew was the right thing to do. *If I don't take my son to practice, will I be letting him down? Will the coach be upset with me?* Unfortunately, I gave in to the enemy of intimidation that day.

Nehemiah's life provides an amazing study of leadership, discernment, and courage. He overcame external as well as any internal turmoil to accomplish the goal of rebuilding the wall.

As I have pondered this scene from my past, I wondered what was the biggest difference between my lack of success and Nehemiah's amazing accomplishments. He was prepared, but I thought I was too, for the most part.

Nehemiah 6:9 held some very important truths for me regarding this.

They were all trying to frighten us, thinking, "Their hands will get too weak for the work, and it will not be completed."

But I prayed, "Now strengthen my hands."

At that moment, Nehemiah needed strength beyond his own. He needed reassurance, direction for the task, and courage. So, what did he do? He simply asked God for His strength.

How easy is that?

It is sometimes hard to filter out all the well-meaning voices and stay the course. Nehemiah teaches us to follow through with God's plan despite difficulty. He is the perfect example of how to have the courage to finish what we know in our hearts to be true.

What I am trying to tell you through example in my own life is that it is important to accomplish and complete your goal. No matter what adversity or challenge faces you, don't waver. Ask God for His strength and guidance.

Set Yourself Up for Success

Here's the challenge for each of us: it is important to set yourself up for success. How? By taking your relationship with God a step further. You do this by partnering with Him in *all* you do throughout each day. Don't wait until your back is up against the wall to invite God into a problem or situation. Remember, what looks good to the world may not be the perfect plan for you or your relationships.

Is there a distraction, enemy, or circumstance that is making you question your decisions about your identity or destiny?

Like my situation, maybe what you're walking through is something you thought you were prepared to handle but are finding out that isn't the case. It could be friend dramas, endless work frustrations, marriage problems, or kid trials. Maybe, like Nehemiah, others are even trying to discourage you and push you to fail. Or maybe you have been battling your own distracting thoughts or those of popular opinion.

Whatever your specific situation, how will you stay the course? How will you take courage? What will you do when you are tired of feeling pushed or pressured? Paul reminds us of the importance of perseverance in 2 Thessalonians 3:13, "Brothers and sisters, don't ever grow weary in doing what is right."

If you are like me, a question about the application of this statement is realistic: How does *not getting tired of doing the right thing* actually work? In the midst of a hard battle, sometimes it feels like it would be easier to give up. I definitely felt that way when my marriage was failing. And I had the same temptation when my husband had cancer.

But I discovered that the only way to persevere was to find that unexplainable strength beyond my own. That's what Nehemiah and I ultimately had in common. We knew where our courage would come from.

The times when I get cynical and discouraged usually turn out to be times when I have lost sight of what I was called to do or lost confidence in who I really am. My worth is not in what I can do, who I know, how well I am liked, or how prepared I can be for life. The key to preparing me for the difficult challenges ahead is in tapping in to that strength beyond my own.

Prepare for the Challenges Ahead

We will always have challenges. There will always be an emergency you can't prepare enough for or didn't plan out. What separates the people who make it from the ones who don't are those who lean into God and partner with Him for supernatural courage.

One of the best things you can do to stay the course is to remain open to the possibility of distractions taking you off the right path. Recognize when others or even your own thoughts and emotions are trying to persuade you to believe something you know is not true.

Most importantly, when you become aware of unsolicited influence, walk through the same steps as Nehemiah.

- Believe in what you're doing and keep going.
- Have courage and stand up to adversity.
- Ask for strength and wisdom.

When the coach called me, I could have easily said, "I'm sorry you feel distressed about the game. But we have looked at the weather, and it is not safe for us to drive to the field today. We will plan to see you when the streets are cleared." I could have been firm, clear, and gracious at the same time. Other situations may find you saying something like, "I am not ready to make a decision yet. Let me pray about it and get back to you."

Like the story of Nehemiah, your goals may be noble. Maybe the more noble the goal, the more opposition we can expect. Can you think of anything more noble than personal restoration? A sound mind, a joyful life?

People may try to persuade you to veer off course, just like they did with him. The voices of dream crushers, naysayers, and self-doubt will emerge. And you will be tempted to listen. You could start to wonder if maybe they're right. Their negative voices might be saying things like, "Why should this work for you?" or "You've tried to change before, just accept who you are." You might begin to believe you are losing the struggle.

But let me encourage you with something I've seen happen time and time again: the biggest breakthroughs, important flashes of insight, and moments of brilliance often occur in those moments when you really want to give up.

In the Song of Songs 5:9, the bride is beginning to see her identity through the trials. She has lived through wounding and pruning (Song of Songs 2:11). She has had the fortitude to endure the adversity of friends' betrayals (5:7), and many of life's traumatic circumstances (4:16). In verse 16, she cries for the north wind to be awakened and do its adverse work in her. The north wind is cold and biting and sure to change her heart in ways she does not understand. In verse 5:9, the maidens address the Shulamite as more beautiful than all the others. They can see His identity shining on her. His identity is becoming hers.

Then, in 6:11 she tells us,

I decided to go down to the valley streams where the orchards of the king grow and mature. I longed to know if hearts were opening. Are the budding vines blooming with new growth? Has their springtime and passionate love arrived?

She has done the hard work of growing and maturing into the person she was created to be. She has taken time to recognize and overcome some of her own weaknesses, and now she is looking for new growth in others and herself. She has found the courage to persevere. She has learned how to love herself and others well.

As a counselor, I often find that courage is the first step toward change. When you are stuck, you need to be reminded to follow what you already know to be true deep inside yourself. Sometimes that means resisting what you hear from others. It means speaking back to the negative thoughts, remembering what you believe, and asking for strength and wisdom to navigate challenges when they come. And they *will* come. No matter how much you prepare, challenges are a part of life. So why not decide now who you are going to listen to in the trials?

Step 11 Exercises: Stand Your Ground

1. This week, spend time recognizing a couple of the battles or distractions that are keeping you from changing, or are holding you back from your life goals or assignments. Write them down in your notebook or journal.

As you look at your list, identify the specifics.

- Are your challenges coming from circumstances or people?
- How are those challenges holding you back from doing what you know you need to do or to be?
- What could you do or say to remind yourself to put them in perspective and stay the course? Remember me thinking about the newspaper headlines. What else could you spend your time thinking about or reminding yourself of in those moments?
- How will you lean on God to give you strength and guidance? What would that look like for you? It will be different for everyone. I had a friend who could only get to this place of wisdom in complete silence. I know another person who needs to literally build herself a nest in her living room with a pillow, blanket, water, and notebook.
- What Scriptures can you use to challenge any discouragement you may be feeling?

2. Practice standing your ground.

- This one could be hard, but stick with me for a minute. Pick a controversial topic from today's culture. Make sure it is one that finds people on both sides of the issue. Write down your opinion about the topic, stating clearly what you believe.

- Ask God to give you the courage, strength, and the right words to say in defending your opinion.

- Recruit a friend or confidant, especially one you know is on the opposite side of the topic. Let them know this will be hard, but you are learning to have confidence in your opinions. Their job in helping you with your step of courage is just to be honest. Now, tell them what you believe about the topic.

- For example, what do you feel or believe about tattoos? You may have moral convictions against them, or you may feel they have great artistic qualities. Most people have an opinion. State yours in a kind but firm manner.

- If you feel brave, ask your friend to push a little against your opinion and even talk to you about an alternative point of view. While your goal is to stay the course, be open to learning something new.

- Try to stay true to your opinion and restate what you believe, remaining calm, firm, and kind. Remember the goal is to be courageous with your position, not to win or to be persuaded.

169

- Agree to walk away from the topic if things start to get heated. Remember, this isn't about winning an argument. It is about you having belief and commitment in yourself in the process.

Step 12: Build and Bond

We have become his poetry, a re-created people that will fulfill the destiny he has given each of us, for we are joined to Jesus, the Anointed One. Even before we were born, God planned in advance our destiny and the good works we would do to fulfill it!

Ephesians 2:10

Hey, friends, we made it to the last chapter! But there are a couple of remaining important concepts we need to understand to know who we are. These foundations are critical for healthy living.

You may have already guessed that I believe we are created by a God who knew what we would be like on our best days and on our worst days. He gave us our talents and understands our downfalls. He knew what we would be good at, and what would come with difficulty. But most importantly, He released us on this earth, wanting us to know we are loved and desired. He established a perfect plan for each of our lives. This concept might be difficult to grasp in your present situation, but it is true.

Jeremiah 29:11 (NIV) says: "'For I know the plans I have for you,' declares the LORD, 'plans to prosper you and not to harm you, plans to give you hope and a future.'" Sadly, for many of us, this does not feel true. What may help with this understanding is discovering what a covenant is and why it matters.

Some of you may be saying, "What? What would a covenant have to do with understanding my plan and purpose in life?" Let's take a look at it.

One of the most important things to remember about a covenant is that it is a selfless act. It does not take much to realize we are immersed in a pretty selfish society today. A covenant runs counterculture to so much of what we see playing out in our world.

Bonded Like Glue

An important implication of the term *covenant* means "a coming together." In the Bible, the word *covenant* is translated from Hebrew over three hundred times! When something is repeated this frequently, it is important.

The Old Testament word refers to a type of bond where two or more parties agree to be bound together. In a word, they decide to be indivisible. The general concept meant sticking together like superglue. In Bible times, a covenant was never to be broken. It was such a sacred commitment, the parties involved would pledge to die before dishonoring themselves by breaking their covenant.

In many countries, a vow or covenant is literally more valuable than the lives of those entering into it. In order to seal a covenant agreement, parties may go so far as to exchange their firstborn children. How crazy is that?

How a covenant was formed is just as important as what happened if the rules or boundaries were breached. Some of the many consequences for breaking an Old Testament agreement included infertility, disease, and defeat by your enemy (see Leviticus 26:14–39 and Deuteronomy 28:15–68).

In the Old Testament, when two people would enter a blood covenant, they would go through specific steps to seal the promise. One of the steps involved cutting their palms or wrists and then rubbing their hands or wrists together. This might be where we got the term *blood brothers*. As their blood mingled, the bond would be sealed and enforced. It could never be broken or annulled.

Likewise, a blood covenant with God is an everlasting commitment and connection with Him. However, this New Testament covenant is also special in the sense that God chooses to fulfill both sides of the oath Himself. He is the only one who shed blood. It's outrageous, but we don't have to do anything but accept what has been given to us: a bond with Him that can never be broken. We will talk more about this at the end of the book.

Today, people can sometimes negotiate their way out of contracts, but it does not work that way with a covenant. One huge difference between a contract and covenant is that within a contract, relationships are often based on protecting self, not the bond. If you have been in this type of a connection, you know it can foster misunderstanding and mistrust. Contracts allow the parties involved to look for loopholes and exit clauses and are centered on your rights and protection. The Bible is clearly trying to show us a different model, one where we feel protected, loved, and a forever commitment.

Finding Your God-Given Purpose

In the Bible, there are many commitments, or covenants of promise, that God gives His people. Let's look at a couple that relate specifically to your God-given purpose in life.

> So we are convinced that every detail of our lives is continually woven together for good, for we are his lovers who have been called to fulfill his designed purpose.
>
> Romans 8:28

> Instead, we are God's accomplishment, created in Christ Jesus to do good things. God planned for these good things to be the way that we live our lives.
>
> Ephesians 2:10 CEB

We are told in these verses that our identity is about who we are in a relationship with, not just about our preferences in life. Why does this matter? Because being in this type of bond not only causes you to experience joy, but it also helps you know deep inside who you were created to be.

Remember, the true meaning of covenant is similar to walking in deep intimacy with another person. So, is covenant really the same thing as intimacy?

When people hear the word *intimacy*, many equate it to physical connection or sex. But covenant intimacy is much more than a flesh connection. It involves the mixing of our life with another person's. Intimacy literally means *in-to-me-see*. It is a mingling of souls and a sharing of hearts, which is something we all long for because it's how God made us. We were designed to connect.

To be honest, there are many types of intimacy, including emotional, spiritual, and physical. Today, the facet of our identity that has many people confused is the physical or sexual component.

One of the big questions is: Were we created male and female? Was this part of our ultimate design? Let's explore this.

Genesis 1 and 2 in the Bible show us the ideal in marriage is a union between two different biological sexes. Why does this matter? One of the reasons is because we were told to multiply on the earth, which can only happen when babies are conceived with a husband (male) and a wife (female). Conception needs the joining of parts from two opposite sexes to create a baby.

At the inception of man's existence, God said:

"Let us make mankind in our image, in our likeness. . . ."
So God created mankind in his own image, in the image of God he created them; male and female he created them. . . .
God saw all that he had made, and it was very good.

Genesis 1:26-27, 31 NIV

This fact is perhaps mankind's greatest claim to fame: We are created in God's image. We all bear His likeness, and He proclaims the model of who we are to be *good*.

Right after creating man in His image, Father God states that man would be better off with a partner. So He created Eve from Adam's side. What happened next signifies the importance of the covenant. Adam tells God he will call her woman because she is bone of his bone and flesh of his flesh. Did you catch that? Adam proclaimed he and Eve are one—they have the same flesh and bone.

Genesis 2:24 (AMP) tells us, "For this reason a man shall leave his father and his mother, and shall be joined to his wife; and they shall become one flesh."

The God of the universe is who created us—and modeled us as either a man or a woman. It tells us man and woman would be united in a blood covenant. This covenant was to be conceived on the marriage night and sealed in blood. In fact, in New Testament times, they would wait to collect the marriage bedsheets to make sure this covenant happened. It sounds sort of creepy and weird to us, but the concept is understood. This bond was to be sealed for all to see and agree with the marriage.

Man and woman were also created to procreate and be fruitful.

God blessed them and said to them, "Be fruitful and increase in number; fill the earth and subdue it. Rule over the fish in the sea and the birds in the sky and over every living creature that moves on the ground."

Genesis 1:28 NIV

God created sex, and He meant it to be fun and fruitful. This blood covenant was intended to be a lifelong relationship, that included offspring. This plan was an expression of the ultimate model of Father God's physical identity for us. The picture of marriage helps us understand God's desire for covenant intimacy with us. That deep connection is a part of who we are—spirit, soul, and physical beings.

In our current culture, our sexual identities have become the thing people are exploring without boundaries, to try to discover their individuality. The problem with this view is it narrows our identity to only being physical. Yes, our sexual identity is one part of who we are, but should it be our entire identity?

You Are More Than a Physical Being

The fact is that humans are amazing and so much more than just physical beings. It is insulting to tie up our identity in only one dimension.

A lot has happened in the world since the sexual revolution of the 1960s. Along with newfound sexual freedoms, we have seen an increase in many things that are not forward-thinking. There has been a massive jump in pornography, sex trafficking, and the number of people deciding against marriage and divorcing with little reason.

We are told some children first view porn around eight years old. Research says it is more addictive than cocaine and relationally and psychologically harmful.[1]

In our culture today, these "new freedoms" can carry the effects of emotional abandonment and trauma for many people. In our lifetime, one-third of marriages will be affected by infidelity. This has had several societal impacts, including an increase in single-parent homes.

The invention of birth control was supposed to give us the choice to take back our lives and bodies and improve our quality of sex. But here is the hard question: Are people truly flourishing in their physical intimacy, or are they more broken, depressed, anxious, and feeling lost and abandoned? The rates of these mental illnesses have climbed globally by more than 25 percent since 2020 alone.[2]

So, is it possible that this revolution, this doing "my own thing," has not caused the freedom we hoped for in society? Today it is very common to sleep with someone on a first date and get to know them later. Is that really connecting with someone at the in-to-me-see level and feeling the safety and comfort of that connection?

We must ask ourselves: Statistically, psychologically, and socially, has the sexual freedom movement met the goal it set out to accomplish? Or has it crushed many people into a life of torment and disillusionment? We now know this independence has resulted in chains of addictions and behaviors that deeply hurt and cause potential shame.[3]

I think there may be a better blueprint for how we are to flourish as human beings. This includes the reality that our identities are much greater than our sexual preferences.

I contend that walking in a covenant is the only thing that brings us true freedom as humans. Because covenant involves boundaries. And the absence of boundaries is not freedom at all—it is the opposite. To have perfect freedom, we must also have some rules. Otherwise, we have chaos. Consider traffic rules in this category. We have the freedom to go or drive almost anywhere we desire, but this comes with the boundaries of respecting other vehicles, state safety rules, and pedestrians. We agree with these rules when we get our licenses.

When we appreciate the importance of a covenant in our lives, then we realize our bodies, minds, and spirits function much better under His design. From the beginning, this covenant was a gift of protection and an instruction manual for love.

Covenant or Relationship?

Covenants are meant to be *lifelong, faithful* relationships. Those are two words that we need to remember when making a covenant commitment. The goal is to be in this relationship until one of you is no longer on this earth.

Covenant partners take responsibility for their actions. When there are difficulties, partners remember their commitment and take responsibility to make things right. Covenant marriages are not built on coercion, deceit, and manipulation. In covenant, we are no longer two, but one.

Covenants are based on commitment, not feelings or thoughts. Because we are human, our feelings are forever fluctuating. They can be subject to what we hear or see from others, the internet, news, or social media. This is not a solid base for our dedication. In covenant, we are faithful to our choices in good times and in bad.

Covenant partners are trustworthy and loyal to their relationships. They will stick with us even when we are not at our best. They speak well of us behind our backs. They are someone we can trust with our lives.

A covenant is identified by

- How may I serve you?
- What can I give?
- I'll give you 100 percent plus.

Relationship is often identified by

- How can you serve me?
- What do I get?
- I'll only do 50 percent at best.

God wants us to love all people. He wants us all to feel perfect, lasting love, which includes people struggling with their emotional, physical, and sexual identities. Culture, including the Church, has often not done this "perfect love" very well. But our goal is to love others as we love ourselves.

It is important to remember that there is a difference between us having temptations to walk outside of the protection of God's rules and actually acting on those impulses. Having a same-sex attraction does not mean this is your identity. Struggling with *any* life temptation doesn't become your identity, and it definitely does not mean that God does not love you. His covenant love for us is unconditional.

Jesus was gracious to people who fell short of God's authority or plan. He will do the same for each of us as we continue to work on the choices in our lives. It is the kindness of God that leads people to a relationship with Him. The Bible promises that God will always give us a way out of the enticements of life.

We all experience times of testing, which is normal for every human being. But God will be faithful to you. He will screen and filter the severity, nature, and timing of every test or trial you face so that you can bear it. And each test is an opportunity to trust him more, for along with every trial God has provided for you a way of escape that will bring you out of it victoriously.

1 Corinthians 10:13

Gentle, Guiding Authority

The definition of the word *authority* comes from the word *author*. God is the ultimate authority of the world and the Author of us. What does God do with His authority? He sends His Son and others to love us and give us rules and boundaries to live by. He offers us a covenant of safety, promise, and love.

He doesn't use His authority to control, pressure, and harshly judge. He gave us each free will. He chose not to dominate us but to guide our choices. Therefore, in order to understand that love, we each need to seek His perfect plan. And then we must follow it.

In Song of Songs 8:6, the bridegroom is telling his bride:

Fasten me upon your heart as a seal of fire forevermore. This living, consuming flame will seal you as my prisoner of love. My passion is stronger than the chains of death and the grave, all consuming as the very flashes of fire from the burning heart of God. Place this fierce, unrelenting fire over your entire being.

Consuming flame? Prison of love? What in the world is this telling us? In this final chapter of the Song of Songs, the bride is now at the place where her groom is telling her that he will be the one to take care of her. He plans to cover her completely in his love.

In biblical times, a seal was used to guarantee the security or indicate ownership. People would place wax seals on letters, scrolls, and important documents. Each seal featured a unique and distinct mark. Only the person who was authorized (or given the authority) to open the document could break the seal. When it was opened, whatever the paper contained or said was as good as done. (Interestingly, if you weren't given authority and still broke this type of seal, it was serious enough to mean imprisonment or even death.)

The seal of fire mentioned in verse 8 was given to the bride for protection, promise, approval, and favor. At this point, she knows she belongs to the groom. She is, by love, under His authority. God is our Author, but His seal of authority is never forced. When we receive it, an imprint is made inside us. The Hebrew word for *seal* can also be translated as "a prison cell." The Lord is trying to imprison us in His love.

His Seal of Love

How do we receive His seal of love over our hearts? We do this by truly getting to know Him, not just know *of* Him. This seal of love will protect us from people who want to harm us. His love will shield us, even from fears of the grave. His love will give us direction into what is good for us, and He does that through our following the authority of His covenant.

The first thing we are told about God in the Bible is that He is the Creator. And we are His creation. As the Author of the universe, we are under His authority. If you are a parent, you understand you have authority since you had a big part in creating your child. Parents want the best for their children and understand better than anyone the need to help them make healthy choices.

Is it possible there is a God who created us, knows everything about us, and has given us guidelines because He wants the best of everything for us because of His love for us?

When I met Charlotte, she was in a same-sex relationship with another woman. She did not feel good about her choices but loved feeling loved. Who doesn't? She described a series of relationships where men had abused and abandoned her throughout her life. As painful as it was for her to live through the discussion of her past and present choices, she sadly felt she deserved her current heartache and the pain that had brought her into my office. Through many conversations and lots of love, she started to understand her value. We dealt with rejection, shame, guilt, and several episodes of hurt and trauma.

When we know God's acceptance and great love, we can start to understand that He is trying to protect us by giving us parameters for our choices. It is important to remember He also provides help and courage when we are tempted to break His guidelines.

It might be difficult to follow God's path of rules. It could mean going a very different direction than all your friends are going, just like Jill from chapter 1. But I would ask you, has doing it your own way made you feel better and more loved? There is a wide road that is easy but leads to destruction, and then there is this narrow and possibly difficult road.

God has called us to that narrow road, which is an intimate, covenant relationship with Him.

In this commitment, He has promised to stand together with us, remain loyal to us, and love us forever, no matter what. That may not sound like any of your relationships in the past, and that is why it is so different. Take a moment to consider the importance and possibility of allowing yourself to be sealed by His covenant love.

Transformative Love and Grace

In my times of adversity, I solidly discovered that God chose each of us. He sees the beauty inside us long before we do. He continually works to help us walk in this unshakeable truth and provides us a way through life's imperfection and pain. He will never leave us or forsake us. His promises will never fail.

After Neal and I nearly lost everything, there was still an aftermath of emotion that had to be addressed. There were many fears that needed to be uncovered, dealt with, and even destroyed. In our struggle to find a place of trust and peace again, we often measured God's grace by human standards. How could God fully heal and forgive? How would we learn to trust again?

The battles were often relentless in my mind, but during those times I clung to a few of God's amazing provisions, like "We have the mind of Christ" (1 Corinthians 2:16 NIV) and "Peace I leave with you; my peace I give you. I do not give to you as the world gives. Do not let your hearts be troubled and do not be afraid" (John 14:27 NIV).

I took a risk when I decided to walk back into my marriage. And I took another to be vulnerable and trust God with the process. With both choices, I reaped a huge reward of freedom. I can tell you now that it was worth it. As it turns out, all my fears were lies.

We both chose to follow the Father's Word over the world's opinion, with "Be kind and compassionate to one another, forgiving each other, just as in Christ God forgave you" (Ephesians 4:32 NIV). We both chose to stop offense in its tracks and throw it out of our house for good.

Because we chose this road, our covenant was restored! Neither of us has to live in the pain and frustration of fear or rejection. In fact, we walk together in joy with healthy thoughts (sound minds) daily.

What's in a Name?

When we were naming our sons, we were very intentional about their names and the definitions of their names. We knew much less than we do now, but we understood these meanings spoke to their identities. When our third son was born, we called him Jacob. Jake questioned his name choice when he got a little older. You see, his name means "supplanter" or "deceiver." Jacob from the Bible comes out of the womb grasping his older brother's heel, and manipulates his older brother into selling his birthright. But here's what we learn when reading Jacob's entire story: God redeems him. God uses him to rescue His chosen people. In fact, God changed his name from Jacob to Israel, which means *God fights*. This is what we were looking at when we named our son Jacob. True to form, our son is a fighter and has an amazing gift of long-suffering when he knows something is worth fighting for.

The act of naming in the Bible demonstrates authority. When God created man, one of the first jobs He gave Adam was to give names to everything under his care. While naming is tied to authority in the Scriptures, it also reveals intimacy. Naming during that time, and today, is in the context of relationships. When you name someone, it shows intimate knowledge—a relationship and privilege.

Consider a few of the following thoughts God had about each of us as He decided our names: fearfully and wonderfully made (Psalm 139:14), known (Jeremiah 1:5), loved (John 3:16), His child (1 John 3:2), predestined (Romans 8:29), adopted (Ephesians 1:5), not forgotten (Isaiah 44:21), no longer orphans (John 14:18), chosen (Ephesians 2:10), forgiven (Luke 1:77–78), heirs (Romans 8:17), God's special possession (1 Peter 2:9), brothers, sisters, sons, daughters, and the bride of Christ (Revelation 21:9)—just to name a few.

So, let me ask you: Who do you think you are?

Unless you haven't realized it yet, let me help you out: You are His beloved, unrivaled in beauty and beyond comparison. Your brokenness is beautiful and in no way excludes you from this covenant relationship.

How to Experience Covenant in Relationships

Everyone is neurologically hardwired to bond, first with God and then with others, which is the place of true intimacy. The word *intimacy* describes a blending of our heart with another so we can "see into" who they really are, and they can "see into" us.

As we've seen, the model for covenant in relationships goes much deeper than the contract many normally follow.

- A contract is based on legalism and leverage.
- A covenant is based on love and loyalty.
- A contract lasts as long as we both shall love.
- A covenant lasts as long as we both shall live.
- A contract calls for the signing of names.
- A covenant calls for the binding of hearts.

Let's be honest. It's a covenant that makes us feel safe and connected with others. Covenant relationships are more than just for marriages and Old Testament prophets. They are for people desiring to experience intimacy and their true identity. Working to understand and experience covenant in relationships is not easy and will challenge anyone on their best day.

The good news is that you will start to experience covenant in your relationships when you work through specific steps to help you with healthier unions.

Three ways to get started with this include revamping prior memories, understanding the dynamics of your relationships, and settling your purpose.

One: Revamping Prior Memories

Previous research has shown that when you imagine something is occurring, it can activate and strengthen the same regions of the brain as if it is currently happening. [4] In other words, you must be careful with your imagination or memory. Focusing on a memory where you were frightened or hurt could bring up the same pain in your mind and body as if it were happening again.

Research also shows it is possible to update your memories by inserting new details.[5] For instance, if you are afraid because you bombed your last piano recital, imagine playing to a standing ovation. If you feel uncoordinated on the pickleball court, imagine the faces of the opponents when you win the match. These activites can boost neuronal connections in regions related to confidence, commitment, and courage.

These studies suggest our imaginations may be a more powerful tool than previously believed for updating and reconstructing memories, especially those that have been hurtful or traumatic. If you have a memory that is crippling you, you can use your imagination to tap in to it, change it, and re-consolidate it.

Revamping how you think about and feel about a past memory can give an old experience new meaning. When you change your story, or alter how you perceive a situation, you are allowing your emotions to experience the possibility of a different outcome. Isn't that amazing?

Pause for a minute to bring up an event that has caused you to wonder about or doubt your passion and purpose. Notice what you feel in your body and emotions when you think about this memory. Write these feelings down as you notice them. After you've done this, you're ready to change the narrative of the situation. Let me give you an example to show you how it works.

Let's say I remember my brother calling me stupid when I was working really hard on a project, and that memory continues to make me feel anxious and worried about my abilities. To change the narrative, I could recall that my brother was really a jerk during that time, and that my parents and friends really liked my project.

Or I could try to imagine what it would have been like if my brother had been a little more thoughtful with his response. What if he had said the project was stupid, but it looked like I'd tried really hard? What would the change in those responses cause me to feel? Try putting those more positive emotions or reactions into your difficult memory.

Two: Understanding the Dynamics of Your Relationships

If it feels like you have never felt love from others, you may also be experiencing a void when it comes to understanding the love of God. However, even with this empty space, know that He is the same God who brings friendship and authority to your life.

It is important to remember that love and authority are not opposites. Both are healthy, offer security, and can coexist in the same person.

Sometimes it is our relationship with our parents or other authority figures that can skew our idea of the word *authority*. How was your relationship with your parents? Was it difficult? Did you struggle believing you were loved and special?

If your family erred on the side of being very rigid and you despised the strictness, you may struggle with authority as being helpful and good. Most likely, you have vowed to be a little more relaxed in life and push against some rules. If it felt like your family didn't show up or even care where you were most of the time, you are probably working hard to understand the need for guidelines. Spend some time being purposeful with this potential struggle in your life.

Consider how you would like to be treated when you are the authority. How would you show this same consideration and honor to others?

Three: Settling Your Purpose

Did you realize that an understanding of covenant relationships also affects your ability to walk in your life purpose? If you don't know who you are, how can you understand what you were created to do and be? Take some time to consider: What do you believe to be true about yourself? Those beliefs drive and influence your relationship with others, as well as everything you do and everything you experience.

There is a verse in the Bible that many scholars have tried to make sense of throughout the generations.

> So Jesus explained, "I tell you the truth, the Son can do nothing by himself. He does only what he sees the Father doing. Whatever the Father does, the Son also does."
>
> John 5:19 NLT

I believe that as Jesus went to the Father in intimacy and covenant, He discovered the details of His daily purpose. He was shown where to go, who to interact with, who to avoid, and where to spend His time. How many of us would love that level of clarity?

We each have the opportunity and privilege to walk with God in similar closeness and understanding. Those instructions that we receive from the Father each day will keep us protected, cause us to walk in freedom and peace, and give joy and meaning to our lives. We can tap in to our creative potential, unleash our talents, and achieve a greater sense of purpose and fulfillment.

Using the example in John 5:19, plan to spend time with the Father, talking with Him about your purpose. Record what He says and reveals to you in these intimate times.

Stepping into the Future

I wrote this book for regular people who are struggling with purpose and maintaining joy in their daily lives. If this is you, I hope you are already starting to experience the reality of restoration. I hope your new normal becomes like that of the bride in the Song of Songs—healthy relationships, hope, healing, and unrelenting affection. You may doubt yourself at first, you may need support as you find your direction in life, you may need encouragement when you fall, but like her, your struggles will be worth it. As you continue following the steps presented here, positive, hope-filled change will happen.

In order to truly move forward, never forget the importance of what you believe, expressed in your thoughts and in your words. Proverbs 23:7 states it plainly, "For as he thinks within himself, so is he." Be intentional about what you think and say over yourself.

Let these words from Romans become a template for a new script for your personal identity: you are entirely accepted, loved, and never abandoned. Read them over and over until your mind, emotions, and spirit settle into the truth of who you really are.

> You did not receive the "spirit of religious duty," leading you back into the fear of never being good enough. But you have received the "Spirit of full acceptance," enfolding you into the family of God. And you will never feel orphaned, for as he rises up within us, our spirits join him in saying the words of tender affection, "Beloved Father!" For the Holy Spirit makes God's fatherhood real to us as he whispers into our innermost being, "You are God's beloved child!"
>
> Romans 8:15–16

Stand strong, friend. You have an identity that is good and sealed in a covenant with your loving Father God.

Step 12 Exercises: Building and Bonding

If you want a better bond with people and with God, try working through the following exercises.

Find a quiet spot without distractions where you can ask God a few questions, and wait for His reply (yes, He desires to talk to you).

1. Ask God: *Could You show me a word, phrase, verse, or picture that helps me to understand my relationship with my parents?* (Feel free to include a different authority figure in your life if you see the need.) Write down the picture/words you see, feel, or hear.

2. After hearing or seeing the answer, ask Him: *Is there anything I need to let go of or anything I need to resolve in this relationship?*

   Most of us will probably hear a yes to this question, but if you do hear a no, skip to step 6.

3. If needed, ask God for clarification on what exactly you need to resolve. Then tell yourself and God that you are willing to let it go and to forgive. Remember, forgiving does not automatically mean reconciliation or excusing what happened.

4. Like you would talk to a friend, tell God exactly who and what you are forgiving. There is no right or wrong way to tell Him about your hurt. Write it down if that helps. Keep working through this step

with each new past hurt that surfaces. If you are not ready to share these hurtful memories and situations with God, try this exercise with a trusted friend or counselor. Let them know you want to move forward with letting go of your pain. (Be patient with yourself, this step could take a while.)

5. Next, ask God to remind you of things that you might have done or said to others for which you need to ask forgiveness. Don't forget to forgive yourself if you have spoken harsh or hateful words.

6. Finally, ask God to show you a word, phrase, verse, or picture that describes how you view your relationship with Him at this moment in time.

   A little hint: if you don't hear something good, go back to step one and make sure you have let go of your hurts. Remember the fact that He can't, by His own design, speak evil over you. Then, continue asking. Don't give up. He will show you something beautiful about your identity.

A SPECIAL INVITATION

No matter where we are in life, we all need a connection to something greater than ourselves. Everyone searches for meaning and purpose that help us understand why we are here and how we should live our lives. This search often leads us to God, the Source of true identity and connection. God is the One who can truly provide us with a sense of belonging and fulfillment. He is the only One who can give us direction and purpose. When we understand this, we can explore and find an intimate relationship with our Creator. We find our true selves in Him, knowing that He will never leave us or forsake us.

If you are unsure of your relationship with God, let me encourage you to call out to Him. Ask Him to show Himself to you. Say something like, *God, I want to experience Your love in my life. Please show me who You are and how You love me. Help me to feel Your presence and get to know You.*

One thing to know about God is that He loved you so much that He sent His only Son to live on this earth, die on the cross for your sins, and rise from the dead. It says in John 3:16 (NIV), "For God so loved the world that he gave his one and only Son, that whoever believes in him shall not perish but have eternal life."

If you believe that and have not yet accepted Jesus into your heart as your personal Savior, now is a good time to do so. Pray this prayer:

Jesus, I believe that You died on the cross for my sins and rose from the dead. I invite You into my life to be my personal Savior. Thank You for forgiving my sins. Help me as I learn to live my life according to the teachings of the Bible. Thank You for my salvation. In Jesus' name, Amen.

If you prayed that prayer, know that I'm rejoicing with you! The next step you'll want to take is to get into a good Bible-based church or group so you can do life in a community with other believers.

I also want to encourage you to read your Bible every day. Start with the book of John. I highly recommend beginning your day in prayer and Bible reading. It may feel awkward at first, but just like any new habit, the more you do it, the easier it will get.

We live in an imperfect world. Many of us have made poor choices or have had to walk through some very difficult things. The good news is that being broken is not your identity. It is the path of learning to find a perfect partner (God) to help us on this journey. God Himself is the only faithful One who will help us to the end.

I hope you will discover this in a greater way in your life. I promise you, it will make the journey one you will never forget or want to change.

God bless you.

ADDITIONAL RESOURCES

If you want to take a deeper dive into who God has called you to be, if you desire more resources, including our courses, or if you find yourself needing community—connect with us at The Family Collective!

The Family Collective takes significant knowledge from science and brings it together with the perfect Word of God. This approach leaves room for the Holy Spirit to move in families and marriages. With the goal to restore, rebuild, and renew personal connections one person at a time, The Family Collective helps individuals and family members realize their unique potential by making healthy relationships a reality. Founders Diane and Neal Arnold, their amazing young adult children, and their talented spiritual children are passionate about restoring others by using lessons from their crises and professional know-how. With support from their global team, they leverage Diane's wisdom of the human brain and behavior, and Neal's deep expertise in family dynamics and business, with the Bible.

The Family Collective focuses on bringing God's perfect covenant design back to the Christian home. We are so thankful for the opportunity every couple, church, and organization give us to work in their vulnerable areas. We know this is not an easy thing to do, and we take it very seriously. On behalf of the whole Family Collective team, we thank you for the chance to walk alongside families, individuals, and married couples to bring about relationships with real and lasting connections.

To learn more about The Family Collective community, courses, groups, books, and resources, visit The Family Collective website at www.thefamilycollective.co.

NOTES

Step 1 Restore the Original Me

1. Amy Novotney, "The Risks of Social Isolation." *Monitor on Psychology* 50, no. 5 (May 2019), https://www.apa.org/monitor/2019/05/ce-corner-isolation.

2. Rebecca Denova, "Zacchaeus," World History Encyclopedia, March 3, 2022, https://www.worldhistory.org/Zacchaeus/.

3. Brian Simmons, *The Sacred Journey: God's Relentless Pursuit of Our Affection* (Savage, MN: Broadstreet Publishing, 2015), 13.

Step 2 Unwrap My Purpose

1. George Barna, *Helping Millennials Thrive: Practical Wisdom for a Generation in Crisis* (Phoenix: Arizona Christian University Press, 2023), 18.

2. George Barna, *Raising Spiritual Champions: Nurturing Your Child's Heart, Mind and Soul* (Tuscon, AZ: Christian University Press and Fedd Books, 2023), 3.

3. Blaise Pascal, *Pensées*, trans. A. J. Krailsheimer (New York: Penguin Books, 1966), 75.

Step 3 Silence Shame

1. Pseudo-orphan syndrome is a group of symptoms experienced by children (and later adults) who were emotionally abandoned. Symptoms include alienation from social life, pathological guilt (stemming from a feeling that they did something wrong and did not deserve love from their parents), anxiety, depression, destructive self-criticism, a neurotic

need for affection and approval (or other types of neurotic needs, like for self-sufficiency), eating and sleep disorders, and addictions.

2. Brené Brown, *Dare to Lead: Brave Work. Tough Conversations. Whole Hearts* (New York: Random House, 2018), 160.

3. Strong's Concordance, s.v. "bosh," Bible Hub, accessed February 6, 2024, https://biblehub.com/hebrew/954.htm.

4. *Strong's Concordance* online, s.v. "thugater," accessed March 18, 2024, https://www.bibletools.org/index.cfm/fuseaction/Lexicon.show/ID/G2364/thugater.htm#:~:text=%CC%81,s%20peculiar%20care%20and%20protection.

5. Brian Simmons, *The Sacred Journey: God's Relentless Pursuit of Our Affection* (Savage, MN: Broadsheet Publishing, 2015), 44.

Step 4 Let in Love and Acceptance

1. Michael L. Slepian, James N. Kirby, Elise K. Kalokerinos, "Shame, Guilt, and Secrets on the Mind," *Emotion* (February 2019), 323–328, accessed online at https://psycnet.apa.org/doiLanding?doi=10.1037%2Femo0000542.

2. Tara Parker-Page, "Are you ready to forgive? A new study shows letting go is good for health," *The Washington Post*, April 20, 2023.

Adam Hamilton, *Forgiveness Leader Guide: Finding Peace Through Letting Go* (Nashville: Abingdon Press, 2018).

Everett Worthington Jr, L. Everett, et al., "Forgiveness in health research and medical practice." *Explore* 1, no. 3 (2005): 169–176.

Step 5 Confront Rejection

1. Kirsten Weir, "The pain of social rejection," *American Psychological Association* 43, no. 4 (2012), https://www.apa.org/monitor/2012/04/rejection.

2. Cigna Big Picture, "New Cigna Study Reveals Loneliness at Epidemic Levels in America," *Cigna*, June 2018, https://www.cignabigpicture.com/issues/june-2018/new-cigna-study-reveals-loneliness-at-epidemic-levels-in-america/.

3. Alexa Lardiere, "Study: Many Americans Report Feeling Lonely, Younger Generations More" U.S. *News and World Report*, May 1, 2018, https://www.usnews.com/news/health-care-news/articles/2018-05-01/study-many-americans-report-feeling-lonely-younger-generations-more-so.

4. Lardiere, "Feeling Lonely."

5. Kristen Weir, "The pain of social rejection," American Psychological Association 43, no. 4 (April 2012): 50.

Michael J. Crowley, Jia Wu, Peter Molfese, Linda C. Mayes, "Social exclusion in middle childhood: rejection events, slow-wave neural activity, and ostracism distress," Social Neuroscience 5, no. 5–6 (2010): 483–95.

6. Robby Berman, "Social isolation, loneliness linked to increased risk of all-cause mortality," Medical News Today, June 27, 2023, https://www.medicalnewstoday.com/articles/social-isolation-loneliness-linked -to-increased-mortality-risk-research-finds.

7. Cigna., "Cigna U.S. Loneliness Index: Survey of 20,000 Americans Examining Behaviors Driving Loneliness in the United States," 2018, https://www.multivu.com/players/English/8294451-cigna-us-loneliness -survey/docs/IndexReport_1524069371598-173525450.pdf.

8. Sarah C. Griffin, Allison B. Williams, Scott G. Ravyts, Samantha N. Mladen, Bruce D. Rybarczyk, "Loneliness and sleep: A systematic review and meta-analysis," Health Psychol Open, April 4, 2020, https://www.ncbi.nlm.nih.gov/pmc/articles/PMC7139193/.

9. Raheel Mushtaq, S. Sheik Shoib, Tabindah Shah, Sahil Mushtaq, "Relationship Between Loneliness, Psychiatric Disorders and Physical health? A Review on the Psychological Aspects of loneliness," Journal of Clinical Diagnostic Research, September 20, 2014, https://www.ncbi .nlm.nih.gov/pmc/articles/PMC4225959/.

10. Jichan J. Kim, Erika S. Payne, Eunjin LeeTracy, "Indirect Effects of Forgiveness on Psychological Health Through Anger and Hope: A Parallel Mediation Analysis," Journal of Religion and Health 61, no. 5 (October 2022): 3729–3746, https://pubmed.ncbi.nlm.nih.gov /35190955/.

11. Renee Onque, "Use these 5 steps to forgive others–it can boost your happiness, says psychologist who studied forgiveness for 30 years" CNBC Make It, May 6, 2023, https://www.cnbc.com/2023/05/06/forgiveness-can -boost-happiness-improve-mental-health-how-to-start.html.

Step 6 Dig New Ditches and Write a Better Story

1. Fran Simone, "Negative Self-Talk: Don't Let It Overwhelm You," *Psychology Today*, December 4, 2017, https://www.psychologytoday.com /gb/blog/family-affair/201712/negative-self-talk-dont-let-it-overwhelm -you.

2. Simone, "Negative Self-Talk."

3. Deepika Choube and Shubham Sharma, "Psychological and Physi-ological Effect in Plant Growth and Health by Using Positive and Nega-tive Words," International Journal of Innovative Research in Technol-ogy 8, no.1 (June 2021), https://www.ijirt.org/master/publishedpaper /IJIRT151445_PAPER.pdf.

Step 7 Navigate Your Loss

1. Jie Zheng, Andrea G. P. Schjetnan, Mar Yebra, Bernard A. Gomes, Clayton P. Mosher, Suneil K. Kalia, Taufik A. Valiante, Adam N. Mamelak, Gabriel Kreiman, and Ueli Rutishauser, "Neurons detect cognitive boundaries to structure episodic memories in humans," National Institutes of Health, U.S. Department of Health and Human Services, March 7, 2022, https://doi.org/10.1038/s41593-022-01020-w.

Step 8 Access Joy in Your Relationships

1. Chris M. Coursey, *The Joy Switch: How Your Brain's Secret Circuit Affects Your Relationship—and How You Can Activate It* (New York: Northfield Publishing, 2021), 30.

2. *Hitchcock's Dictionary of Bible Names*, s.v. "Naomi," accessed March 18, 2024, https://www.biblestudytools.com/dictionaries/hitchcocks-bible-names/naomi.html.

International Standard Bible Encyclopedia, s.v. "Naomi," accessed March 18, 2024, https://www.biblestudytools.com/encyclopedias/isbe/naomi.html.

3. Nicole Spector, "Smiling can trick your brain into happiness—and boost your health," NBC News, January 9, 2018, https://www.nbcnews.com/better/health/smiling-can-trick-your-brain-happiness-boost-your-health-ncna822591.

4. Louie D. Brook, Karolina Brook, Elizabeth Frates, "The Laughter Prescription: A Tool for Lifestyle Medicine," *American Journal of Lifestyle Medicine*, June 23, 2016, https://pubmed.ncbi.nlm.nih.gov/30202281/.

5. "Create Joy and Satisfaction," Mental Health America, accessed January 30, 2024, https://www.mhanational.org/create-joy-and-satisfaction.

Step 9 Who Are You Listening To?

1. Archibald D. Hart, *The Anxiety Cure: You Can Find Emotional Tranquility and Wholeness* (Nashville: Thomas Nelson, 2001), 15.

Step 10 Practice the Discipline of Peace

1. John Paul Jackson, "The Gospel of Peace," Streams Ministries, video, 4:00, June 29, 2012, https://www.youtube.com/watch?v=4ohjsBqgiKs&ab_channel=StreamsMinistries.

2. Jackson, "Gospel of Peace."

Step 12 Build and Bond

1. Rob Jackson, "When Children View Pornography," Focus on the Family Australia, 2004, https://families.org.au/article/when-children-view-pornography/.

2. Sofia Villas-Boas, Soctt Kaplan, Justin S. White, et al, "Patterns of US Mental Health-Related Emergency Department Visits During the COVID-19 Pandemic," JAMA Network, July 11, 2023, https://jamanetwork.com/journals/jamanetworkopen/fullarticle/2807138.

3. Himani Adarsh, Swapnajeet Sahoo, "Pornography and Its Impact on Adolescent/Teenage Sexuality," Journal of Psychosexual Health, 5.1, 35–39, March 9, 2023, https://journals.sagepub.com/doi/10.1177/26318318231153984.

4. University of Colorado at Boulder, "Your Brain on Imagination: It's a Lot like Reality, Study Shows," ScienceDaily, December 10, 2018, https://www.sciencedaily.com/releases/2018/12/181210144943.htm.

5. Colorado at Boulder, "Brain on Imagination."

DIANE ARNOLD is a licensed professional counselor specializing in family and marriage counseling. She is also a certified EFT and EMDR trained therapist. Through her study of relationship attachment, Diane has spoken and written extensively on overcoming trauma and betrayal with remarkable results. She serves on WOFL, Shiloh Company, and National Children's Day boards. Diane is also one of the founders of The Grace Center, an international emotional healing center.

Diane and her husband, Neal, have been married for forty-two years and have three adult children and five grandchildren. They co-authored three books: *Take Heart*, which is a snapshot of attachment theory and the dynamics of healing relationships; *Face to Face*, a marriage training and coaching workbook; and *Face to Face Pre-Marital*, a premarital training and preparation workbook. With Neal's support, Diane wrote *12 Habits for a Sound Mind and Joyful Life* to provide a journey of understanding for readers to uncover their identity and purpose in life. Through their family nonprofit, The Family Collective, Diane and Neal continue to write and speak on the foundational importance of family and local community connections in building healthy businesses, cities, and countries. Learn more at TheFamilyCollective.co.